Mathcounts State Compe

Volume 3

http://www.mymathcounts.com/index.php

This book can be used by 6th to 8th grade students preparing for Mathcounts State and National Competitions. Each chapter consists of (1) basic skill and knowledge section with plenty of examples, (2) exercise problems, and (3) detailed solutions to all problems.

Mathcounts is a nationwide middle school mathematics competition held in the United States. Mathcounts program is open to sixth, seventh, and eighth grade students. The competition is divided into four stages: school, chapter, state, and national.

We would like to thank the Mathcounts for their mathematical ideas and problems. We cited a few problems directly from these tests but provided our own solutions.

We would also like to thank the following students who kindly reviewed the manuscripts and made valuable suggestions and corrections: Maximus Lu (New York), Prakash Alladi (MA), Alix Cui (NE), Priyo Majumdar (LA), Skyler Wu (CA), Christina Yu, (CA), Claire Zhang (MA), Lizzie Zhou (VA), Rubin Zou (NH).

ISBN-13: 978-1505241389
ISBN-10: 1505241383

Please contact mymathcounts@gmail.com for suggestions, corrections, or clarifications.

Table of Contents

This page is intentionally left blank.

BASIC KNOWLEDGE

Below is a list of useful formulas to be aware of and know. They can all be derived through expanding or factoring.

Perfect square trinomial

$$(x+y)^2 = x^2 + 2xy + y^2 \qquad\qquad (x+y)^2 = (x-y)^2 + 4xy$$

$$(x-y)^2 = x^2 - 2xy + y^2 \qquad\qquad (x-y)^2 = (x+y)^2 - 4xy$$

$$(x+y)^2 + (x-y)^2 = 2(x^2 + y^2) \qquad (x+y)^2 - (x-y)^2 = 4xy$$

$$(x+y+z)^2 = x^2 + y^2 + z^2 + 2xy + 2xz + 2yz$$

$$x^2 + y^2 + z^2 - xy - yz - zx = \frac{1}{2}[(x-y)^2 + (y-z)^2 + (z-x)^2]$$

$$(x+y+z+w)^2 = x^2 + y^2 + z^2 + w^2 + 2xy + 2xz + 2xw + 2yz + 2yw + 2zw$$

Difference and sum of two squares

$$x^2 - y^2 = (x-y)(x+y) \qquad\qquad x^2 + y^2 = (x-y)^2 + 2xy$$

$$x^2 + y^2 = (x+y)^2 - 2xy \qquad\qquad x^2 + \frac{1}{x^2} = (x + \frac{1}{x})^2 - 2$$

Difference and sum of two cubes

$$x^3 - y^3 = (x-y)(x^2 + xy + y^2)$$
$$x^3 + y^3 = (x+y)(x^2 - xy + y^2)$$

1

$$x^3 + \frac{1}{x^3} = (x+\frac{1}{x})[(x+\frac{1}{x})^2 - 3] = (x+\frac{1}{x})^3 - 3(x+\frac{1}{x})$$

$$(x+y)^3 = x^3 + 3x^2y + 3xy^2 + y^3 = x^3 + y^3 + 3xy(x+y).$$

$$(x-y)^3 = x^3 - 3x^2y + 3xy^2 - y^3 = x^3 - y^3 - 3xy(x-y).$$

Sum of two numbers of the fourth power

$$(x+y)^4 = x^4 + 4x^3y + 6x^2y^2 + 4xy^3 + y^4$$

$$(x-y)^4 = x^4 - 4x^3y + 6x^2y^2 - 4xy^3 + y^4$$

$$x^4 + y^4 = (x+y)^4 - 4xy(x+y)^2 + 2(xy)^2$$

$$x^4 + \frac{1}{x^4} = (x+\frac{1}{x})^4 - 4(x+\frac{1}{x})^2 + 2$$

Other formulas

$$x^n - y^n = (x-y)(x^{n-1} + x^{n-2}y + \cdots + y^{n-1})$$ for all n.

$$x^n - y^n = (x+y)(x^{n-1} - x^{n-2}y + \ldots - y^{n-1})$$ for all even n.

$$x^n + y^n = (x+y)(x^{n-1} - x^{n-2}y + \ldots + y^{n-1})$$ for all odd n.

$$(1-x)(1+x+x^2+x^3+\cdots+x^{n-1}) = 1 - x^n.$$

PROBLEM SOLVING SKILLS

1. Calculations

Example 1. What is the value of $\dfrac{(2015^2 - 2014) \times 2016}{2015^2 - 2015 \times 2014 + 2014^2}$?

Solution: 2016.

Let 2015 be x.

$$\frac{[x^2 - (x-1)] \times (x+1)}{x^2 - x \times (x-1) + (x-1)^2} = \frac{(x^2 - x + 1) \times (x+1)}{x^2 - x^2 + x + x^2 - 2x + 1} = \frac{(x^2 - x + 1) \times (x+1)}{x^2 - x + 1} = x + 1$$

$$\frac{(2015^2 - 2014) \times 2016}{2015^2 - 2015 \times 2014 + 2014^2} = 2015 + 1 = 2016.$$

Example 2. (2014 National Sprint Round) What is the value of

$$\frac{2013^3 - 2 \cdot 2013^2 \cdot 2014 + 3 \cdot 2013 \cdot 2014^2 - 2014^3 + 1}{2013 \cdot 2014} \, ?$$

Solution: 2013.

Note: $(a - b)^3 = a^3 - 3 \cdot a^2 \cdot b + 3 \cdot a \cdot b^2 - b^3$.

$$\frac{2013^3 - 2 \cdot 2013^2 \cdot 2014 + 3 \cdot 2013 \cdot 2014^2 - 2014^3 + 1}{2013 \cdot 2014}$$

$$= \frac{2013^3 - 3 \cdot 2013^2 \cdot 2014 + 3 \cdot 2013 \cdot 2014^2 - 2014^3 + 2013^2 \cdot 2014 + 1}{2013 \cdot 2014}$$

$$= \frac{(2013 - 2014)^3 + 2013^2 \cdot 2014 + 1}{2013 \cdot 2014} = \frac{-1 + 2013^2 \cdot 2014 + 1}{2013 \cdot 2014} = \frac{2013^2 \cdot 2014}{2013 \cdot 2014}$$

$= 2013.$

Example 3. (2011 Mathcounts State Sprint Problem 30) What is the value of
$52{,}683 \times 52{,}683 - 52{,}660 \times 52{,}706$?

Solution: 529.

Let 52,683 be x.

$52,683 \times 52,683 - 52,660 \times 52,706 =$

$x^2 - (x-23)(x+23) = x^2 - (x^2 - 23^2) = 23^2 = 529$.

Example 4. Compute $(2014 \times 2018)^2 - 2 \times 2016^2 - 2013 \times 2015 \times 2017 \times 2019$.

Solution: 7.

Let 2016 be x.

$[(n-2)(n+2)]^2 - 2n^2 - (n-3)(n-1)(n+1)(n+3)$

$= (n^2 - 4)^2 - 2n^2 - (n^2 - 9)(n^2 - 1)$

$= n^4 - 8n^2 + 16 - 2n^2 - n^4 + 10n^2 - 9 = 7$.

Example 5. Compute $\dfrac{20162015^2}{20162014^2 + 20162016^2 - 2}$.

Solution: 1/2.

Let 20162015 be n.

$$\frac{20162015^2}{20162014^2 + 20162016^2 - 2} = \frac{n^2}{(n-1)^2 + (n+1)^2 - 2}$$

$$= \frac{n^2}{n^2 - 2n + 1 + n^2 + 2n + 1 - 2} = \frac{n^2}{2n^2} = \frac{1}{2}$$

Example 6. Calculate $(2+1)(2^2+1)(2^4+1)\cdots(2^{32}+1)+1$.

Solution: 2^{64}.

Notice that $(2-1)(2+1) = 2^2 - 1$.

We multiply the given expression by $1 = 2 - 1$:

$$[(2-1)(2+1)](2^2+1)(2^4+1)\cdots(2^{32}+1)+1=[(2^2-1)(2^2+1)](2^4+1)\cdots(2^{32}+1)+1$$
$$=[(2^8-1)(2^8+1)(2^{16}+1)...(2^{32}+1)]+1$$
$$=(2^{32}-1)(2^{32}+1)+1=2^{64}-1+1=2^{64}.$$

Example 7. If $m=(1+2^{-\frac{1}{64}})(1+2^{-\frac{1}{32}})(1+2^{-\frac{1}{16}})(1+2^{-\frac{1}{8}})(1+2^{-\frac{1}{4}})(1+2^{-\frac{1}{2}})$, then m is equal to

(A) $\dfrac{1}{2}(1-2^{-\frac{1}{64}})^{-1}$ (B) $(1-2^{-\frac{1}{64}})^{-1}$ (C) $1-2^{-\frac{1}{64}}$ (D) $\dfrac{1}{2}(1-2^{-\frac{1}{64}})$ (E) $\dfrac{1}{2}$

Solution: (A). $\dfrac{1}{2}(1-2^{-\frac{1}{64}})^{-1}$.

Let $x=2^{-\frac{1}{64}}$.
Then $m=(1+x)(1+x^2)(1+x^4)(1+2^8)(1+x^{16})(1+x^{32})$ (1)
We multiply both sides of (1) by $(1-x)$:
$(1-x)m=(1-x)(1+x)(1+x^2)(1+x^4)(1+x^8)(1+x^{16})(1+x^{32})$ $\Rightarrow$
$(1-x)m=(1-x^2)(1+x^2)(1+x^4)(1+x^8)(1+x^{16})(1+x^{32})$ $\Rightarrow$
$(1-x)m=(1-x^4)(1+x^4)(1+x^8)(1+x^{16})(1+x^{32})$ $\Rightarrow$
$(1-x)m=(1-x^8)(1+x^8)(1+x^{16})(1+x^{32})$ $\Rightarrow$
$(1-x)m=(1-x^{16})(1+x^{16})(1+x^{32})$ $\Rightarrow$

$(1-x)m=(1-x^{32})(1+x^{32})=1-x^{64}=1-(2^{-\frac{1}{64}})^{64}=1-\dfrac{1}{2}=\dfrac{1}{2}$

$m=\dfrac{1}{2(1-x)}=\dfrac{1}{2(1-2^{-\frac{1}{64}})}=\dfrac{1}{2}(1-2^{-\frac{1}{64}})^{-1}$.

Example 8. Find the positive integer value of x if
$$\frac{x^{19}+x^{18}+x^{17}+\cdots+x^2+x+1}{x^9+x^8+x^7+\cdots+x^2+x+1}=1025.$$

Solution: 2.

$$\frac{x^{19}+x^{18}+x^{17}+\cdots+x^2+x+1}{x^9+x^8+x^7+\cdots+x^2+x+1}$$

$$=\frac{(1-x)(x^{19}+x^{18}+x^{17}+\cdots+x^2+x+1)}{(1-x)(x^9+x^8+x^7+\cdots+x^2+x+1)}=\frac{1-x^{20}}{1-x^{10}}=\frac{(1-x^{10})(1+x^{10})}{1-x^{10}}=1+x^{10}.$$

Thus $1+x^{10}=1025 \quad \Rightarrow \quad x^{10}=1024=2^{10}$.

The positive integer value is $x=2$.

Example 9. Calculate $(\frac{1}{2}+\frac{1}{3}+\cdots\frac{1}{2015})\,(1+\frac{1}{2}+\frac{1}{3}+\cdots\frac{1}{2014})\,-$

$(1+\frac{1}{2}+\frac{1}{3}+\cdots\frac{1}{2015})\,(\frac{1}{2}+\frac{1}{3}+\cdots\frac{1}{2014})$.

Solution: $\dfrac{1}{2015}$.

Let $m=(\frac{1}{2}+\frac{1}{3}+\cdots\frac{1}{2015})$ and $n=(\frac{1}{2}+\frac{1}{3}+\cdots\frac{1}{2014})$.

The original expression becomes:

$$m(1+n)-(1+m)n=m+mn-n-mn=m-n$$

$$=(\frac{1}{2}+\frac{1}{3}+\cdots\frac{1}{2015})-(\frac{1}{2}+\frac{1}{3}+\cdots\frac{1}{2014})=\frac{1}{2015}.$$

2. Formulas Applications

Example 10. The difference of two positive integers is 34 and the product is 2015. What is the sum of the squares of them?

Solution: 5186.

Method 1:

Let the two numbers be x and y.

We have

$x - y = 34$ (1)
$xy = 2015$ (2)

We square both sides of (1): $(x - y)^2 = 34^2$ $\Rightarrow$ $x^2 - 2xy + y^2 = 34^2$ (3)
$2 \times$ (2): $2xy = 2 \times 2015$. (4)
Substituting (4) into (3): $x^2 - 2 \times 2015 + y^2 = 34^2$ $\Rightarrow$ $x^2 + y^2 = 34^2 + 2 \times$ 2015 = 5186.

Method 2:
$2015 = 5 \times 403 = 5 \times 13 \times 31 = 31 \times 65$.
$65 - 31 = 34$.
So the two numbers are 31 and 65. $31^2 + 65^2 = 5186$.

Example 11. If $xy = b$ and $\dfrac{1}{x^2} + \dfrac{1}{y^2} = a$, find $(x - y)^2$. Express your answer in terms of a and b.

Solution: $ab^2 - 2b$ or $b(ab - 2)$.

$\dfrac{1}{x^2} + \dfrac{1}{y^2} = \dfrac{x^2 + y^2}{(xy)^2} = a.$ So $x^2 + y^2 = ab^2$.

$x^2 + y^2 = ab^2$ can be written as $x^2 + y^2 - 2xy = ab^2 - 2xy$ $\Rightarrow$
$$(x - y)^2 = ab^2 - 2b = b(ab - 2).$$

Example 12. If $x = 2014$, $y = 2015$, and $z = 2016$, what is the value of $x^2 + y^2 + z^2 - xy - yz - zx$?

Solution: 3.
$x^2 + y^2 + z^2 - xy - yz - zx$
$= \dfrac{1}{2}(2x^2 + 2y^2 + 2z^2 - 2xy - 2yz - 2zx)$

$$= \frac{1}{2}[(x^2 - 2xy + y^2) + (y^2 - 2yz + z^2) + (z^2 - 2zx + x^2)]$$

$$= \frac{1}{2}[(x-y)^2 + (y-z)^2 + (z-x)^2]$$

$$= \frac{1}{2}[(2004 - 2015)^2 + (2015 - 2016)^2 + (2016 - 2014)^2]$$

$$= \frac{1}{2}[(-1)^2 + (-1)^2 + (2^2)] = 3.$$

Example 13. If $x = 2014a + 2015$, $y = 2014a + 2016$, and $z = 2014a + 2017$, what is the value of $x^2 + y^2 + z^2 - xy - yz - zx$?

Solution: 3.
$x - y = (2014a + 2015) - (2014a + 2016) = -1.$
$y - z = -1.$
$z - x = 2.$

$x^2 + y^2 + z^2 - xy - yz - zx$

$$= \frac{1}{2}[(x-y)^2 + (y-z)^2 + (z-x)^2]$$

$$= \frac{1}{2}[(-1)^2 + (-1)^2 + (2^2)] = 3.$$

Example 14. If $a - b = 2 + \pi$, $b - c = 2 - \pi$, what is the value of $a^2 + b^2 + c^2 - ab - bc - ca$? Express your answer in terms of π.

Solution: $12 + \pi^2$.
$a - b = 2 + \pi,$
$b - c = 2 - \pi,$
$c - a = c - b - (a - b) = \pi - 2 - (2 + \pi) = -4.$
.

$a^2 + b^2 + c^2 - ab - bc - ca$

$= \dfrac{1}{2}[(a-b)^2 + (b-c)^2 + (c-a)^2]$

$= \dfrac{1}{2}[(2+\pi)^2 + (2-\pi)^2 + (-4)^2]$

$= 12 + \pi^2.$

Example 15. Find the value of $xy + yz + zx$ if $x + y + z = 0$ and $x^2 + y^2 + z^2 = 1$. Express your answer as a common fraction.

Solution: $-\dfrac{1}{2}$.

We know that $(x+y+z)^2 = x^2 + y^2 + z^2 + 2xy + 2xz + 2yz$.

We are given that $x + y + z = 0$ and $x^2 + y^2 + z^2 = 1$, so

$0 = 1 + 2(xy + yz + zx)$ $\Rightarrow$ $xy + yz + zx = -\dfrac{1}{2}.$

Example 16. If $x - y = a$, and $z - y = 10$, what is the smallest value of $x^2 + y^2 + z^2 - xy - yz - zx$?

Solution: 75.

We know that $x - y = a$, and $z - y = 10$. So $z - x = (z-y) - (x-y) = 10 - a.$

$x^2 + y^2 + z^2 - xy - yz - zx$

$= \dfrac{1}{2}[(x-y)^2 + (y-z)^2 + (z-x)^2]$

$= \dfrac{1}{2}[a^2 + 10^2 + (10-a)^2]$

$= a^2 - 10a + 100$

$= (a-5)^2 + 75$

When $a = 5$, the smallest value is 75.

Example 17. What is the smallest value of $x^2 + x + \dfrac{1}{8}$ if x is real? Express your answer as a common fraction.

Solution: $-\dfrac{1}{8}$.

$$x^2 + x + \frac{1}{8} = x^2 + 2x \times \frac{1}{2} + (\frac{1}{2})^2 - (\frac{1}{2})^2 + \frac{1}{8} = (x + \frac{1}{2})^2 - \frac{1}{4} + \frac{1}{8} = (x + \frac{1}{2})^2 - \frac{1}{8}$$

We know that for any real number, $(x + \dfrac{1}{2})^2 \geq 0$. The smallest value of

$x^2 + x + \dfrac{1}{8}$ is $-\dfrac{1}{8}$ when $x = -\dfrac{1}{2}$.

Example 18. What is the greatest value of u if $13x^2 - 6xy + y^2 - 4x + u = 0$? Both x and y are real.

Solution: 1.

$13x^2 - 6xy + y^2 - 4x + u = 0 \Rightarrow (3x - y)^2 + (2x - 1)^2 + u - 1 = 0$

$1 - u = (3x - y)^2 + (2x - 1)^2 \geq 0$. So $u \leq 1$.

Since both x and y are real

$(3x - y)^2 \geq 0$

$(2x - 1)^2 \geq 0$

When $3x - y = 0$ and $2x - 1 = 0$, i.e. $x = \dfrac{1}{2}$, and $y = \dfrac{3}{2}$, u has the greatest value 1.

Example 19. Find the value of ab if $a^2 - 2ab + 2b^2 + 4a + 8 = 0$. Both a and b are real numbers.

Solution: 8.

We multiply the given equation by 2: $2a^2 - 4ab + 4b^2 + 8a + 16 = 0$ $\Rightarrow$

$(a^2 - 4ab + 4b^2) + (a^2 + 8a + 16) = 0 \Rightarrow$

$(a - 2b)^2 + (a + 4)^2 = 0$.

Since $(a - 2b)^2 \geq 0$ and $(a + 4)^2 \geq 0$, we have $(a - 2b)^2 = 0$ and $(a + 4)^2 = 0$.

So $a = -4$ and $b = \dfrac{1}{2}a = -2$.

Therefore $ab = (-4) \times (-2) = 8$.

Example 20. (2010 National Sprint Round Problem 30) If x and y are positive real numbers for which $(x + y)^2 + (x - y)^2 = 10$ and $(x + y)^4 + (x - y)^4 = 98$, what is the value of xy? Express your answer in simplest radical form.

Solution: $\sqrt{6}$.

Method 1:

Expand $(x + y)^2 + (x - y)^2$ to get

$x^2 + 2xy + y^2 + x^2 - 2xy + y^2 = 2(x^2 + y^2) = 10 \rightarrow x^2 + y^2 = 5$.

Square both sides to get

$(x^2 + y^2)^2 = x^4 + 2x^2 y^2 + y^4 = 25$.

Expand $(x + y)^4 + (x - y)^4 = 98$ to get

$(x^4 + 4x^3 y + 6x^2 y^2 + 4xy^3 + y^4) + (x^4 - 4x^3 y + 6x^2 y^2 - 4xy^3 + y^4) = 98 \qquad \Rightarrow$

$2x^4 + 12x^2 y^2 + 2y^4 = 98 \Rightarrow x^4 + 6x^2 y^2 + y^4 = 49 \Rightarrow$

$x^4 + 2x^2 y^2 + y^4 + 4(xy)^2 = 49 \Rightarrow 25 + 4(xy)^2 = 49$

$\Rightarrow 4x^2 y^2 = 24 \Rightarrow x^2 y^2 = 6$.

Since x and y are positive real numbers, $xy = \sqrt{6}$.

Method 2:

Expand $(x + y)^2 + (x - y)^2$ to get

$x^2 + 2xy + y^2 + x^2 - 2xy + y^2 = 2(x^2 + y^2) = 10 \rightarrow x^2 + y^2 = 5$.

$$x^2 + 2xy + y^2 = 5 + 2xy \qquad \Rightarrow \qquad (x+y)^2 = 5 + 2xy \qquad (1)$$

$$x^2 - 2xy + y^2 = 5 - 2xy \qquad \Rightarrow \qquad (x-y)^2 = 5 - 2xy \qquad (2)$$

Squaring both sides of (1): $(x+y)^4 = (5+2xy)^2 = 25 + 4x^2y^2 + 20xy$ \qquad (3)

Squaring both sides of (2): $(x-y)^4 = (5-2xy)^2 = 25 + 4x^2y^2 - 20xy$ \qquad (4)

(3) + (4): $(x+y)^4 + (x-y)^4 = 50 + 8x^2y^2$ or $50 + 8x^2y^2 = 98 \Rightarrow 8x^2y^2 = 48$

$$\Rightarrow x^2y^2 = 6.$$

Since x and y are positive real numbers, $xy = \sqrt{6}$.

3. Simplifying Rational Expressions

Example 21. If $x^2 - 6x + 1 = 0$, what is the value of $x^2 + \dfrac{1}{x^2}$?

Solution: 34.

We know that $x \neq 0$. So we divide both sides of the equation by x: $x - 6 + \dfrac{1}{x} = 0$

$$\Rightarrow \qquad x + \frac{1}{x} = 6.$$

$$x^2 + \frac{1}{x^2} = (x + \frac{1}{x})^2 - 2 = 36 - 2 = 34.$$

Example 22. Find $m^2 + \dfrac{1}{m^2}$ if $m + \dfrac{1}{m} = 4$.

Solution: 14.

Method 1:

Since $(x+y)^2 = x^2 + 2xy + y^2$, we have:

$$x^2 + y^2 = (x+y)^2 - 2xy \qquad (1)$$

Let $x = m$ and $y = \dfrac{1}{m}$ in (1): $m^2 + \dfrac{1}{m^2} = \left(m + \dfrac{1}{m}\right)^2 - 2m \times \dfrac{1}{m} = 4^2 - 2 = 14$.

Method 2:

$$m^2 + \frac{1}{m^2} = m^2 + 2 - 2 + \frac{1}{m^2} = m^2 + 2 \times m \times \frac{1}{m} - 2 + \frac{1}{m^2}$$

$$= [m^2 + 2 \times m \times \frac{1}{m} + (\frac{1}{m})^2] - 2 = \left(m + \frac{1}{m}\right)^2 - 2 = 4^2 - 2 = 14.$$

Example 23. (2014 Mathcounts State Sprint Problem 21) If $x^2 + \frac{1}{x^2} = 3$ and $x > 0$, what is the value of $x + \frac{1}{x}$? Express your answer in simplest radical form.

Solution: $\sqrt{5}$.

We re-write $x^2 + \frac{1}{x^2} = 3$ as $x^2 + \frac{1}{x^2} = x^2 + 2 \times x \times \frac{1}{x} + (\frac{1}{x})^2 - 2 = (x + \frac{1}{x})^2 - 2 = 3$

$$\Rightarrow \qquad (x + \frac{1}{x})^2 = 5.$$

Since $x > 0$, $x + \frac{1}{x} = \sqrt{5}$.

Example 24. Find $m^3 + \frac{1}{m^3}$ if $m + \frac{1}{m} = 2$.

Solution: 2.
Method 1:

Multiplying both sides of $m + \frac{1}{m} = 2$ by m yields

$$m^2 + 1 = 2m \quad \Rightarrow \quad m^2 - 2m + 1 = 0 \quad \Rightarrow \quad (m-1)^2 = 0.$$
Solving this equation, we get $m = 1$.

Therefore $m^3 + \frac{1}{m^3} = 1^3 + \frac{1}{1^3} = 1 + 1 = 2$.

Method 2:

We know that $(x+y)^3 = x^3 + 3x^2y + 3xy^2 + y^3 = x^3 + y^3 + 3xy(x+y)$.

So $x^3 + y^3 = (x+y)^3 - 3xy(x+y)$ $\hspace{4cm}$ (1)

Substituting in $x = m$ and $y = \dfrac{1}{m}$ into (1) gives us:

$$m^3 + \frac{1}{m^3} = (m + \frac{1}{m})^3 - 3m \times \frac{1}{m}(m + \frac{1}{m}) = 2^3 - 3 \times 2 = 2.$$

Method 3:

We know that $x^3 + y^3 = (x+y)(x^2 - xy + y^2)$.

Substituting $x = m$ and $y = \dfrac{1}{m}$ into the above equation, we get:

$$m^3 + \frac{1}{m^3} = (m + \frac{1}{m})(m^2 - m \cdot \frac{1}{m} + \frac{1}{m^2}) = 2[(m + \frac{1}{m})^2 - 3] = 2(2^2 - 3) = 2$$

Method 4:

Multiplying both sides of $m + \dfrac{1}{m} = 2$ by $(m^2 + \dfrac{1}{m^2} - 1)$ yields

$$(m^2 + \frac{1}{m^2} - 1)(m + \frac{1}{m}) = 2(m^2 + \frac{1}{m^2} - 1) \quad \Rightarrow \quad m^3 + \frac{1}{m^3} =$$

$$2[(m + \frac{1}{m})^2 - 2 - 1] = 2.$$

Example 25. (2003 Mathcounts State Sprint Problem 30) If $x + \dfrac{1}{x} = 4$, then what is the value of $x^3 + \dfrac{1}{x^3}$?

Solution: 52.

We know that $x^3 + \dfrac{1}{x^3} = (x + \dfrac{1}{x})^3 - 3(x + \dfrac{1}{x}) = 4^3 - 3 \times 4 = 64 - 12 = 52$.

The answer is 52.

Example 26. (2002 Mathcounts National Sprint) If $a + b = 7$ and $a^3 + b^3 = 42$, what is the value of the sum $\dfrac{1}{a} + \dfrac{1}{b}$? Express your answer as a common fraction.

Solution: 21/43.

$$\frac{a^3 + b^3}{a + b} = \frac{(a+b)(a^2 - ab + b^2)}{a + b} = (a^2 - ab + b^2), \text{ or}$$

$$a^2 - ab + b^2 = 6 \tag{1}$$
$$(a+b)^2 = 7^2 \qquad \Rightarrow \qquad a^2 + 2ab + b^2 = 49 \tag{2}$$

Subtracting (1) from (2), we get: $ab = \dfrac{43}{3}$

So $\dfrac{1}{a} + \dfrac{1}{b} = \dfrac{a+b}{ab} = \dfrac{7}{\dfrac{43}{3}} = \dfrac{21}{43}$

Example 27. Find $m^4 + \dfrac{1}{m^4}$ if $m + \dfrac{1}{m} = 4$.

Solution: 194.

Substituting m^2 for x and $\dfrac{1}{m^2}$ for y into $x^2 + y^2 = (x + y)^2 - 2xy$ gives us:

$$m^4 + \frac{1}{m^4} = \left(m^2 + \frac{1}{m^2}\right)^2 - 2 = \left[\left(m + \frac{1}{m}\right)^2 - 2\right]^2 - 2 = (16 - 2)^2 - 2 = 194.$$

Example 28. Find $m^4 + \dfrac{1}{m^4}$ if $m - \dfrac{1}{m} = 4$. Express your answer in the simplest radical form.

15

Solution: 322.

Substituting m^2 for x and $\dfrac{1}{m^2}$ for y into $x^2 + y^2 = (x-y)^2 + 2xy$ gives us:

$$m^4 + \frac{1}{m^4} = \left(m^2 - \frac{1}{m^2}\right)^2 + 2 = (m - \frac{1}{m})^2(m + \frac{1}{m})^2 + 2 .$$

$$= 16(m + \frac{1}{m})^2 + 2 \qquad\qquad\qquad\qquad (1)$$

Squaring both sides of $m - \dfrac{1}{m} = 4$: $(m - \dfrac{1}{m})^2 = 16 \Rightarrow \left(m^2 + \dfrac{1}{m^2}\right) = 18$.

We also have $\left(m^2 + \dfrac{1}{m^2}\right) = 18 \Rightarrow m^2 + \dfrac{1}{m^2} + 2 = 18 + 2 \qquad \Rightarrow$

$$m^2 + \frac{1}{m^2} + 2m \times \frac{1}{m} = 20 \qquad \Rightarrow \qquad (m + \frac{1}{m})^2 = 20 \qquad \Rightarrow$$

$$(m + \frac{1}{m}) = 2\sqrt{5}$$

Substituting this value into (1): $m^4 + \dfrac{1}{m^4} = 16(m + \dfrac{1}{m})^2 + 2 = 16(2\sqrt{5})^2 + 2$

$$= 16 \times 4 \times 5 + 2 = 322 .$$

Example 29. If $x^2 + \dfrac{1}{x^2} = 7$, then what is the value of $x^4 + \dfrac{1}{x^4}$?

Solution: 47.

Substituting x^2 for x and $\dfrac{1}{x^2}$ for y into $x^2 + y^2 = (x+y)^2 - 2xy$ gives us:

$$x^4 + \frac{1}{x^4} = \left(x^2 + \frac{1}{x^2}\right)^2 - 2 = (7)^2 - 2 = 47 .$$

Example 30. If $x^2 - \dfrac{1}{x^2} = 2$, then what is the value of $x^4 + \dfrac{1}{x^4}$?

Solution: 6.

We know that $x^2 - \dfrac{1}{x^2} = 2$. So $x^4 - 1 = 2x^2 \Rightarrow \qquad x^4 - 2x^2 = 1$ (1)

We also know that $x^2 - \dfrac{1}{x^2} = 2$. So $\dfrac{1}{x^2} = x^2 - 2 \qquad \Rightarrow \qquad \dfrac{1}{x^4} = (x^2 - 2)^2$ (2)

Thus $x^4 + \dfrac{1}{x^4} = x^4 + (x^2 - 2)^2 = x^4 + x^4 - 4x^2 + 4 = 2(x^4 - 2x^2 + 2)$

$= 2(1 + 2) = 6$

4. Simplifying Radicals

Example 31. Find the value of $x^2 + y^2$ if $x = \dfrac{1}{\sqrt{3} + \sqrt{2}}$, and $y = \dfrac{1}{\sqrt{3} - \sqrt{2}}$.

Solution: 10.

$x = \dfrac{1}{\sqrt{3} + \sqrt{2}} = \dfrac{\sqrt{3} - \sqrt{2}}{(\sqrt{3} + \sqrt{2})(\sqrt{3} - \sqrt{2})} = \sqrt{3} - \sqrt{2}$, $y = \dfrac{1}{\sqrt{3} - \sqrt{2}} =$

$\dfrac{\sqrt{3} + \sqrt{2}}{(\sqrt{3} - \sqrt{2})(\sqrt{3} + \sqrt{2})} = \sqrt{3} + \sqrt{2}$.

$x^2 + y^2 = (\sqrt{3} - \sqrt{2})^2 + (\sqrt{3} + \sqrt{2})^2 = (5 - 2\sqrt{3} \times \sqrt{2}) + (5 + 2\sqrt{3} \times \sqrt{2}) = 10$.

Example 32. Find the value of $x^2 + y^2$ if $x = \dfrac{1}{\sqrt{5} + \sqrt{3}}$, and $y = \dfrac{1}{\sqrt{5} - \sqrt{3}}$.

Solution: 4.
Method 1:

$x = \dfrac{1}{\sqrt{5} + \sqrt{3}} = \dfrac{\sqrt{5} - \sqrt{3}}{(\sqrt{5} + \sqrt{3})(\sqrt{5} - \sqrt{3})} = \dfrac{\sqrt{5} - \sqrt{3}}{2}$, $y = \dfrac{1}{\sqrt{5} - \sqrt{3}} =$

$\dfrac{\sqrt{5} + \sqrt{3}}{(\sqrt{5} - \sqrt{3})(\sqrt{5} + \sqrt{3})} = \dfrac{\sqrt{5} + \sqrt{3}}{2}$.

$$x^2 + y^2 = (\frac{\sqrt{5}-\sqrt{3}}{2})^2 + (\frac{\sqrt{5}+\sqrt{3}}{2})^2 = \frac{8-2\sqrt{15}}{4} + \frac{8+2\sqrt{15}}{4} = \frac{16}{4} = 4$$

Method 2:

$$x = \frac{1}{\sqrt{5}+\sqrt{3}} = \frac{\sqrt{5}-\sqrt{3}}{(\sqrt{5}+\sqrt{3})(\sqrt{5}-\sqrt{3})} = \frac{\sqrt{5}-\sqrt{3}}{2}, \ y = \frac{1}{\sqrt{5}-\sqrt{3}} =$$

$$\frac{\sqrt{5}+\sqrt{3}}{(\sqrt{5}-\sqrt{3})(\sqrt{5}+\sqrt{3})} = \frac{\sqrt{5}+\sqrt{3}}{2}.$$

$$x + y = \frac{\sqrt{5}+\sqrt{3}+\sqrt{5}-\sqrt{3}}{2} = \sqrt{5}$$

$$xy = \frac{(\sqrt{5}+\sqrt{3})(\sqrt{5}-\sqrt{3})}{2\times 2} = \frac{2}{4} = \frac{1}{2}$$

$$x^2 + y^2 = (x+y)^2 - 2xy = (\sqrt{5})^2 - 2\times\frac{1}{2} = 5-1 = 4$$

Example 33. Find $m^3 - \frac{1}{m^3}$ if $y = \sqrt{m^2-m-1} + \sqrt{m+1-m^2}$, where both m and y are real numbers.

Solution: 4.

Since y is given to be a real number, the expressions under the square roots must be greater than or equal to 0. Therefore,

$$\begin{cases} m^2 - m - 1 \geq 0 \\ m+1-m^2 \geq 0 \Rightarrow m^2 - m - 1 \leq 0 \end{cases}$$

Since $m^2 - m - 1$ must be both greater than or equal to 0 and less than or equal to 0, $m^2 - m - 1 = 0$ $\Rightarrow$ $m - \frac{1}{m} = 1$ ($m \neq 0$).

$$m^3 - \frac{1}{m^3} = \left(m - \frac{1}{m}\right)\left(m^2 + \frac{1}{m^2} + 1\right) = \left(m - \frac{1}{m}\right)\left[\left(m - \frac{1}{m}\right)^2 + 3\right] = 4.$$

PROLEMS

Problem 1. What is the value of $\dfrac{2015^3 - 2014(2015^2 + 2016)}{2014(2013^2 - 2012) - 2013^3}$?

Problem 2. Find the value of $\dfrac{2016^3 - 2015^3 + 6048 \times 2015^2 - 2016^2 \times 3 \times 2015}{2015^2 + 2016^2 - 2015 \times 4032}$.

Problem 3. What is the value of $2{,}016 \times 2{,}016 - 2{,}017 \times 2{,}015$?

Problem 4. Compute $2013 \times 20152015 - 2015 \times 20132012$.

Problem 5. Compute $\dfrac{1}{2015^3 - 2014(2015^2 + 2016)}$.

Problem 6. What is the value of $\dfrac{2015^3 - 2 \times 2015^2 - 2013}{2015^3 + 2015^2 - 2016}$?

Problem 7. Calculate $(2+1)(2^2 + 1)(2^4 + 1)\cdots(2^{64} + 1) + 1$.

Problem 8. If $n = (1 + 2^{32})(1 + 2^{16})(1 + 2^8)(1 + 2^4)(1 + 2^2)(1 + 2^1)$, then n is equal to

(A) $\dfrac{1}{2}(2^{64} - 1)$ (B) $(2^{64} - 1)$ (C) 2^{64} (D) 2^{63} (E) 2^{48}

Problem 9. Find the real value of $1+x+x^2+x^3+\cdots+x^{2015}$ if $x^3+x^2+x+1=0$.

Problem 10. The difference of two positive integers is 14 and the product is 975. What is the sum of the squares of them?

Problem 11. If $2xy = b$ and $\dfrac{1}{x^2}+\dfrac{1}{y^2}=a$, find $(x+y)^2$. Express your answer in terms of a and b.

Problem 12. If $x = 1990$, $y = 1991$, and $z = 1992$, what is the value of $x^2+y^2+z^2 -- xy - yz -zx$?

Problem 13. If $x = 1999a + 2000$, $y = 1999a + 2001$, and $z = 1999a + 2002$, what is the value of $x^2+y^2+z^2 -xy -yz -zx$?

Problem 14. If $x = 1990a + 1989$, $y = 1990a + 1990$, and $z = 1990a + 1991$, what is the value of $x^2+y^2+z^2 -xy -yz -zx$?

Problem 15. If $x = 2000a + 1998$, $y = 2000a + 1999$, and $z = 2000a + 2000$, what is the value of $x^2+y^2+z^2 -xy -yz -zx$?

Problem 16. If $x + y + z = 0$, and $xy + yz + zx = -\dfrac{1}{2}$, what is the value of $x^2+y^2+z^2$?

Problem 17. What is the smallest value of $x^2 - 6xy + 10y^2 - 2y + 2016$ if both x and y are real?

Problem 18. Find the value of $(8a^3 + 8a^2 + 4a + 1)(8a^3 - 8a^2 + 4a - 1)$ if $a = \dfrac{1}{2}$.

Problem 19. Find the value of $a^2b + ab^2$ if $2a^2 - 2ab + b^2 + 4a + 4 = 0$. Both a and b are rational numbers.

Problem 20. If $x^2 - 3x + 1 = 0$, what is the value of $x^2 + \dfrac{1}{x^2}$?

Problem 21. If $x^2 + \dfrac{1}{x^2} = 6$ and $x < 0$, what is the value of $x + \dfrac{1}{x}$? Express your answer in simplest radical form.

Problem 22. Find $a^3 + \dfrac{1}{a^3}$ if $a + \dfrac{1}{a} = \sqrt{3}$.

Problem 23. Find $m^4 - \dfrac{1}{m^4}$ if $m - \dfrac{1}{m} = 4$. Express your answer in the simplest radical form.

Problem 24. If $x^2 + \dfrac{1}{x^2} = 7$, then what is the positive value of $x^4 - \dfrac{1}{x^4}$? Express your answer in the simplest radical form.

Problem 25. Find $m + n$ if $a^4 + \dfrac{1}{a^4} = m$, $a^4 - \dfrac{1}{a^4} = n$, and $a + \dfrac{1}{a} = -2$.

Problem 26. Find $m^6 + \dfrac{1}{m^6}$ if $m + \dfrac{1}{m} = 4$.

Problem 27. If $a^2 - 3a + 1 = 0$, what is the value of $\dfrac{a^3}{a^6 + 1}$? Express your answer as a common fraction.

Problem 28. (2009 National Sprint Round) If r is a root of $x^2 + 2x - 15 = 0$, what is the greatest possible value of $\dfrac{r^3 - 1}{r^5 + r^4 - r^3 - r^2}$? Express your answer as a common fraction.

Problem 29. (2002 China Middle School Math Contest) What is the value of $\dfrac{a+b}{a-b}$ if $a^2 + b^2 = 4ab$, where $a < b < 0$. Express your answer in the simplest radical form.

Problem 30. Find the value of $\dfrac{y}{x^2} + \dfrac{x}{y^2}$ if $x = \dfrac{\sqrt{3} - \sqrt{2}}{\sqrt{3} + \sqrt{2}}$, and $y = \dfrac{\sqrt{3} + \sqrt{2}}{\sqrt{3} - \sqrt{2}}$.

Problem 31. Find the value of $x^2 + 6xy + y^2$ if $x = \dfrac{\sqrt{5} + \sqrt{3}}{2}$, and $y = \dfrac{\sqrt{5} - \sqrt{3}}{2}$.

Problem 32. Find $r^3 + \dfrac{1}{r^3}$ if $r + \dfrac{1}{r} = \sqrt{2}$.

Problem 33. If $x = \dfrac{3 + \sqrt{13}}{2}$, find the value of $x^2 + \dfrac{1}{x^2}$.

Problem 34. Find the real positive value of x if $\dfrac{x^8 + x^7 + \cdots + x^2 + x + 1}{x^6 + x^3 + 1} = 13$.

SOLUTIONS

Problem 1. **Solution:** 1.

Method 1:

Let 2015 be x and 2013 be y.

$$\frac{x^3 - (x-1)(x^2 + x + 1)}{(y+1)[(y^2 - (y-1)] - y^3} = \frac{x^3 - (x-1)x^2 - (x-1)x + 1)}{(y+1)y^2 - (y+1)(y-1) - y^3}$$

$$= \frac{x^3 - x^3 + x^2 - (x^2 - 1)}{y^3 + y^2 - (y^2 - 1) - y^3} = \frac{x^2 - x^2 + 1}{y^2 - y^2 + 1} = 1$$

So $\dfrac{2015^3 - 2014(2015^2 + 2016)}{2014(2013^2 - 2012) - 2013^3} = 1.$

Method 2:

$$\frac{2015^3 - 2014(2015^2 + 2016)}{2014(2013^2 - 2012) - 2013^3} = \frac{2015^3 - 2014 \times 2015^2 - 2014 \times 2016}{2014 \times 2013^2 - 2014 \times 2012 - 2013^3}$$

$$= \frac{2015^2(2015 - 2014) - 2014 \times 2016}{2013^2(2014 - 2013) - 2014 \times 2012} = \frac{2015^2 - (2015 - 1)(2015 + 1)}{2013^2 - (2013 + 1)(2013 - 1)}$$

$$= \frac{2015^2 - (2015^2 - 1)}{2013^2 - (2013^2 - 1)} = \frac{1}{1} = 1$$

Problem 2. **Solution:** 1.

$$\frac{2016^3 - 2015^3 + 6048 \times 2015^2 - 2016^2 \times 3 \times 2015}{2015^2 + 2016^2 - 2015 \times 4032}$$

$$= \frac{2016^3 - 3 \times 2016^2 \times 2015 + 3 \times 2016 \times 2015^2 - 2015^3}{2016^2 - 2015 \times 4032^2 + 2015^2} = \frac{(2016 - 2015)^3}{(2016 - 2015)^2} = 1$$

Problem 3. **Solution**: 1.

Let 2,016 be x.

$2{,}016 \times 2{,}016 - 2{,}017 \times 2{,}015 = x^2 - (x+1)(x-1) = x^2 - (x^2 - 1) = 1$

Problem 4. Solution: 2015.

Let 2013 be n.

The original expression becomes:

$n[(n+2)\times10^4 +(n+2)]-(n+2)[n\times10^4 +(n-1)]$

$= n(n+2)\times10^4 +n(n+2)-n(n+2)\times10^4 -(n+2)(n-1)]$

$= n(n+2)-(n+2)(n-1)] = n(n+2)-n(n+2)+(n+2)=n+2$

$= 2013 + 2 = 2015.$

Problem 5. Solution: 1.

Let 2015 be x.

$$\frac{1}{2015^3 -2014(2015^2 +2016)} = \frac{1}{x^3 -(x-1)(x^2 +x+1)}$$

$$= \frac{1}{x^3 -(x-1)x^2 -(x-1)(x+1)} = \frac{1}{x^3 -x^3 +x^2 -(x^2 -1)} = \frac{1}{x^2 -x^2 +1}=1.$$

Problem 6. Solution: $\dfrac{671}{672}$.

Method 1:

$$\frac{2015^3 -2\times2015^2 -2013}{2015^3 +2015^2 -2016} = \frac{2015^2(2015-2)-2013}{2015^2(2015+1)-2016}$$

$$= \frac{2015^2(2013)-2013}{2015^2(2016)-2016} = \frac{2013(2015^2 -1)}{2016(2015^2 -1)} = \frac{2013}{2016} = =\frac{671}{672}.$$

Method 2:

Let n be 2015.

$$\frac{n^3 -2n^2 -n-2}{n^3 +n^2 -n-1} = \frac{n^2(n-2)-n-2}{n^2(n+1)-(n+1)} = \frac{(n-2)(n^2 -1)}{(n+1)(n^2 -1)} = \frac{n-2}{n+1} = \frac{2013}{2016} = \frac{671}{672}.$$

Problem 7. Solution: 2^{128}.

Notice that $(2-1)(2+1) = 2^2 -1.$

We multiply the given expression by $1 = 2 - 1$:

$$[(2-1)(2+1)](2^2+1)(2^4+1)\cdots(2^{64}+1)+1 = [(2^2-1)(2^2+1)](2^4+1)\cdots(2^{64}+1)+1$$

$$= [(2^8-1)(2^8+1)(2^{16}+1)\cdots(2^{64}+1)]+1$$

$$= (2^{64}-1)(2^{64}+1)+1 = 2^{128}-1+1 = 2^{128}.$$

Problem 8. Solution: (B). $(2^{64}-1)$.

Let $y = 2$.

Then $n = (1+y)(1+y^2)(1+y^4)(1+y^8)(1+y^{16})(1+y^{32})$ (2)

We multiply both sides of (1) by $(1-y)$:

$$(1-y)n = (1-y)(1+y)(1+y^2)(1+y^4)(1+y^8)(1+y^{16})(1+y^{32}) \quad \Rightarrow$$

$$(1-y)n = 1 - y^{64} \quad \Rightarrow \quad (1-y)n = 1 - (2)^{64}.$$

$$n = \frac{1-2^{64}}{1-y} = 2^{64}-1 .$$

Problem 9. Solution: 0.

$$x^3 + x^2 + x + 1 = 0 \quad \Rightarrow \quad (x+1)(x^2+1) = 0.$$

We know that $x^2 + 1 \neq 0$. Thus $x + 1 = 0$.

$$1 + x + x^2 + x^3 + \cdots + x^{2015} = 1 - 1 + 1 - 1 + \cdots + 1 - 1 = 0$$

Problem 10. Solution: 2146.

Method 1:

Let the two numbers be x and y.

We have

$x - y = 14$ (1)

$xy = 975$ (2)

We square both sides of (1): $(x-y)^2 = 14^2 \quad \Rightarrow \quad x^2 - 2xy + y^2 = 14^2$ (3)

$2 \times$ (2): $2xy = 2 \times 975$ (4)

Substituting (4) into (3): $x^2 - 2 \times 975 + y^2 = 14^2 \quad \Rightarrow \quad x^2 + y^2 = 14^2 + 2 \times 975 = 2146$.

Method 2:

Let the two numbers be x and y.

We have $x - y = 14$ and $xy = 975$

$x^2 + y^2 = (x - y)^2 + 2xy = 14^2 + 2 \times 975 = 2146$.

Method 3:

$975 = 25 \times 39$.

$39 - 25 = 14$.

So the two numbers are 39 and 625. $39^2 + 25^2 = 2146$.

Problem 11. **Solution:** $ab^2 + b$ or $b(ab + 1)$

$$\frac{1}{x^2} + \frac{1}{y^2} = \frac{x^2 + y^2}{(xy)^2} = a. \text{ So } x^2 + y^2 = ab^2.$$

$x^2 + y^2 = ab^2$ can be written as $x^2 + y^2 + 2xy = ab^2 + 2xy \Rightarrow$

$$(x + y)^2 = ab^2 + b = b(ab + 1).$$

Problem 12. **Solution:** 3.

$x^2 + y^2 + z^2 - xy - yz - zx$

$$= \frac{1}{2}(2x^2 + 2y^2 + 2z^2 - 2xy - 2yz - 2zx)$$

$$= \frac{1}{2}[(x^2 - 2xy + y^2) + (y^2 - 2yz + z^2) + (z^2 - 2zx + x^2)]$$

$$= \frac{1}{2}[(x - y)^2 + (y - z)^2 + (z - x)^2]$$

$$= \frac{1}{2}[(1990 - 1991)^2 + (1991 - 1992)^2 + (1992 - 1990)^2]$$

$$= \frac{1}{2}[(-1)^2 + (-1)^2 + (2^2)] = 3.$$

Problem 13. **Solution:** 3.

$x - y = -1.$

$y - z = -1.$

$z - x = 2.$

$x^2 + y^2 + z^2 - xy - yz - zx = \dfrac{1}{2}[(x-y)^2 + (y-z)^2 + (z-x)^2]$

$= \dfrac{1}{2}[(-1)^2 + (-1)^2 + (2^2)] = 3.$

Problem 14. Solution: 3.

$x - y = -1.$

$y - z = -1.$

$z - x = 2.$

$x^2 + y^2 + z^2 - xy - yz - zx = \dfrac{1}{2}[(x-y)^2 + (y-z)^2 + (z-x)^2]$

$= \dfrac{1}{2}[(-1)^2 + (-1)^2 + (2^2)] = 3.$

Problem 15. Solution: 3.

$x - y = -1.$

$y - z = -1.$

$z - x = 2.$

$x^2 + y^2 + z^2 - xy - yz - zx = \dfrac{1}{2}[(x-y)^2 + (y-z)^2 + (z-x)^2]$

$= \dfrac{1}{2}[(-1)^2 + (-1)^2 + (2^2)] = 3.$

Problem 16. Solution: 1.

We know that $(x + y + z)^2 = x^2 + y^2 + z^2 + 2xy + 2xz + 2yz$.

$0 = x^2 + y^2 + z^2 + 2(xy + xz + yz) \Rightarrow 0 = x^2 + y^2 + z^2 + 2(\dfrac{1}{2}) \Rightarrow x^2 + y^2 + z^2 = -1.$

Problem 17. Solution: 2015.

29

$$x^2 - 6xy + 10y^2 - 2y + 2016 = (x^2 - 6xy + 9y^2) + (y^2 - 2y + 1) + 2015$$
$$= (x - 3y)^2 + (y - 1)^2 + 2015.$$

Since both x and y are real

$$(x - 3y)^2 \geq 0$$

$$(y - 1)^2 \geq 0$$

When $x - 3y = 0$ and $y - 1 = 0$, i,e, $y = 1$, and $x = 3y = 3$,

$x^2 - 6xy + 10y^2 - 2y + 2016$ has the smallest value 2015.

Problem 18. **Solution:** 0.

$$(8a^3 + 8a^2 + 4a + 1)(8a^3 - 8a^2 + 4a - 1)$$
$$= [(8a^3 + 4a) + (8a^2 + 1)][(8a^3 + 4a) - (8a^2 + 1)]$$
$$= (8a^3 + 4a)^2 - (8a^2 + 1)^2$$
$$= 64a^6 + 64a^4 + 16a^2 - 64a^4 - 16a^2 - 1$$
$$= 64a^6 - 1 = 64 \times (\frac{1}{2})^6 - 1 = 1 - 1 = 0$$

Problem 19. **Solution:** -16.

The original equation can be written as $(a^2 - 2ab + b^2) + (a^2 + 4a + 4) = 0 \Rightarrow$

$$(a - b)^2 + (a + 2)^2 = 0.$$

Since $(a - b)^2 \geq 0$ and $(a + 2)^2 \geq 0$, we have $(a - b)^2 = 0$ and $(a + 2)^2 = 0$.

So $a = -2$ and $b = a = -2$.

Therefore $a^2b + ab^2 = (-2)^2 \times (-2) + (-2) \times (-2)^2 = -16$.

Problem 20. **Solution:** 7.

We know that x is not a solution of the equation. So $x \neq 0$. So we divide both sides

of the equation by x: $x - 3 + \dfrac{1}{x} = 0 \quad \Rightarrow \quad x + \dfrac{1}{x} = 3$.

$x^2 + \dfrac{1}{x^2} = (x + \dfrac{1}{x})^2 - 2 = 9 - 2 = 7$.

Problem 21. Solution: $-2\sqrt{2}$.

We re-write $x^2 + \dfrac{1}{x^2} = 6$ as $x^2 + \dfrac{1}{x^2} = (x + \dfrac{1}{x})^2 - 2 = 6 \qquad \Rightarrow (x + \dfrac{1}{x})^2 = 8$.

Since $x < 0$, $x + \dfrac{1}{x} = -\sqrt{8} = -2\sqrt{2}$.

Problem 22. Solution: 0.

$a^3 + \dfrac{1}{a^3} = \left(a + \dfrac{1}{a}\right)^3 - 3\left(a + \dfrac{1}{a}\right) = 3\sqrt{3} - 3\sqrt{3} = 0$.

Problem 23. Solution: $144\sqrt{5}$.

Squaring both sides of $m - \dfrac{1}{m} = 4$: $(m - \dfrac{1}{m})^2 = 16 \quad \Rightarrow \left(m^2 + \dfrac{1}{m^2}\right) = 18$.

We also have $\left(m^2 + \dfrac{1}{m^2}\right) = 18 \Rightarrow m^2 + \dfrac{1}{m^2} + 2 = 18 + 2 \qquad \Rightarrow$

$m^2 + \dfrac{1}{m^2} + 2m \times \dfrac{1}{m} = 20 \Rightarrow \quad (m + \dfrac{1}{m})^2 = 20 \qquad \Rightarrow \qquad (m + \dfrac{1}{m}) = 2\sqrt{5}$.

$m^4 - \dfrac{1}{m^4} = \left(m^2 - \dfrac{1}{m^2}\right)\left(m^2 + \dfrac{1}{m^2}\right) = 18\left(m^2 - \dfrac{1}{m^2}\right) = 18(m - \dfrac{1}{m})(m + \dfrac{1}{m})$

$= 18 \times 4 \times 2\sqrt{5} = 144\sqrt{5}$.

Problem 24. Solution: $21\sqrt{5}$.

We know that $x^2 + \dfrac{1}{x^2} = 7$. So $x^2 + \dfrac{1}{x^2} + 2 = 7 + 2 \Rightarrow x^2 + \dfrac{1}{x^2} + 2 \times x \times \dfrac{1}{x} = 9 \Rightarrow$

$(x + \dfrac{1}{x})^2 = 9 \Rightarrow \qquad (x + \dfrac{1}{x}) = 3$ or $(x + \dfrac{1}{x}) = -3$

Similarly, $(x - \dfrac{1}{x}) = \sqrt{5}$ or $(x - \dfrac{1}{x}) = -\sqrt{5}$

$$x^4 - \frac{1}{x^4} = \left(x^2 + \frac{1}{x^2}\right)\left(x^2 - \frac{1}{x^2}\right) = 7\left(x^2 - \frac{1}{x^2}\right) = 7(x - \frac{1}{x})(x + \frac{1}{x}).$$

Since we want the positive value, w have

$$x^4 - \frac{1}{x^4} = 7(x - \frac{1}{x})(x + \frac{1}{x}) = 7 \times \sqrt{5} \times 3 = 21\sqrt{5}.$$

Problem 25. Solution: 2.

Substituting a^2 for x and $\frac{1}{x^2}$ for y into $x^2 + y^2 = (x + y)^2 - 2xy$ gives us:

$$a^4 + \frac{1}{a^4} = \left(a^2 + \frac{1}{a^2}\right)^2 - 2 = \left[\left(a + \frac{1}{a}\right)^2 - 2\right]^2 - 2 = \left(4 - 2\right)^2 - 2 = 2 \qquad (1)$$

Squaring both sides of (1): $(a^4 + \frac{1}{a^4})^2 = 4 \quad \Rightarrow \quad a^8 + \frac{1}{a^8} + 2 = 4 \qquad \Rightarrow$

$$a^8 + \frac{1}{a^8} = 2 \quad \Rightarrow \quad a^8 + \frac{1}{a^8} - 2 = 2 - 2 \quad \Rightarrow$$

$$(a^4)^2 + \frac{1}{(a^4)^2} - 2a^4 \times \frac{1}{a^4} = 0 \quad \Rightarrow \quad (a^4 - \frac{1}{a^4})^2 = 0 \Rightarrow \quad a^4 - \frac{1}{a^4} = 0.$$

The answer is $2 + 0 = 2$.

Problem 26. Solution: 2702.

We know that $m^2 + \frac{1}{m^2} = \left(m + \frac{1}{m}\right)^2 - 2 = 4^2 - 2 = 14.$

$$m^6 + \frac{1}{m^6} = \left(m^2 + \frac{1}{m^2}\right)\left(m^4 + \frac{1}{m^4} - 1\right)$$

$$= \left(m^2 + \frac{1}{m^2}\right)\left[\left(m^2 + \frac{1}{m^2}\right)^2 - 3\right] = 14\left(14^2 - 3\right) = 2702.$$

Problem 27. Solution: $\frac{1}{18}$.

We know that $a^2 - 3a + 1 = 0$. So $a \neq 0$. We divide both sides of the equation by

A: $a - 3 + \dfrac{1}{a} = 0$ $\Rightarrow$ $a + \dfrac{1}{a} = 3$.

Let $m = \dfrac{a^3}{a^6 + 1}$. Then $\dfrac{1}{m} = \dfrac{a^6 + 1}{a^3} = a^3 + \dfrac{1}{a^3} = (a + \dfrac{1}{a})(a^2 - a \times \dfrac{1}{a} + \dfrac{1}{a^2})$

$= 3(a^2 + \dfrac{1}{a^2} - 1) = 3[(a + \dfrac{1}{a})^2 - 2 - 1] = 3[(3)^2 - 3] = 18$.

So $m = \dfrac{1}{18}$.

Problem 28. Solution: $\dfrac{13}{144}$.

The two roots for the quadratic equation $x^2 + 2x - 15 = 0$ are $r = -5$ and $r = 3$.

$$\frac{r^3 - 1}{r^5 + r^4 - r^3 - r^2} = \frac{(r-1)(r^2 + r + 1)}{r^4(r+1) - r^2(r+1)} = \frac{(r-1)(r^2 + r + 1)}{(r+1)r^2(r+1)(r-1)} = \frac{(r^2 + r + 1)}{(r+1)^2 r^2}$$

If r is 3, we get: $\dfrac{(r^2 + r + 1)}{(r+1)^2 r^2} = \dfrac{(3^2 + 3 + 1)}{(3+1)^2 3^2} = \dfrac{13}{144}$

If r is -5, we get: $\dfrac{(r^2 + r + 1)}{(r+1)^2 r^2} = \dfrac{(-5)^2 - 5 + 1}{(-5+1)^2 5^2} = \dfrac{21}{400}$

The greatest possible value is $\dfrac{13}{144}$.

Problem 29. Solution: $\sqrt{3}$.

Adding $2ab$ to both sides of the original equation: $a^2 + b^2 + 2ab = 4ab + 2ab$ or
$(a + b)^2 = 6ab$.

Since $a < b < 0$, $a + b < 0$. So $a + b = -\sqrt{6ab}$ (1)

Subtracting $2ab$ from both sides of the original equation:

$a^2 + b^2 - 2ab = 4ab - 2ab$ or $(a - b)^2 = 2ab$

Since $a < b < 0$, $a - b < 0$. $\Rightarrow$ $a - b = -\sqrt{2ab}$ (2)

$(1) \div (2)$: $\dfrac{a+b}{a-b} = \dfrac{-\sqrt{6ab}}{-\sqrt{2ab}} = \sqrt{3}$.

Problem 30. Solution: 970.

$xy = 1$, and $x + y = (\sqrt{3} - \sqrt{2})^2 + (\sqrt{3} - \sqrt{2})^2 = 10$

$\dfrac{y}{x^2} + \dfrac{x}{y^2} = \dfrac{x^3 + y^3}{(xy)^2} = \dfrac{(x+y)(x^2 - xy + y^2)}{(xy)^2} = \dfrac{(x+y)[(x+y)^2 - 3xy]}{(xy)^2}$

$= 10(10^2 - 3) = 970$.

Problem 31. Solution: 7.

$x = \dfrac{\sqrt{5} + \sqrt{3}}{2}$, $y = \dfrac{\sqrt{5} - \sqrt{3}}{2}$.

$x + y = \dfrac{\sqrt{5} + \sqrt{3} + \sqrt{5} - \sqrt{3}}{2} = \sqrt{5}$ and $xy = \dfrac{(\sqrt{5} + \sqrt{3})(\sqrt{5} - \sqrt{3})}{2 \times 2} = \dfrac{2}{4} = \dfrac{1}{2}$

$x^2 + +6xy + y^2 = (x + y)^2 + 4xy = (\sqrt{5})^2 + 4 \times \dfrac{1}{2} = 5 + 2 = 7$.

Problem 32. Solution: $-\sqrt{2}$.

We know that $r^3 + \dfrac{1}{r^3} = \left(r + \dfrac{1}{r}\right)\left(r^2 - 1 + \dfrac{1}{r^2}\right)$, and $\left(r + \dfrac{1}{r}\right)^2 = r^2 + 2 + \dfrac{1}{r^2} = 2$.

The second equation gives us $r^2 + \dfrac{1}{r^2} = 0 \Rightarrow r^2 - 1 + \dfrac{1}{r^2} = -1$.

Therefore, $r^3 + \dfrac{1}{r^3} = (r + \dfrac{1}{r})(-1) = -\sqrt{2}$.

Problem 33. Solution: 11.

$x^2 + \dfrac{1}{x^2} = x^2 - 2x\dfrac{1}{x} + \dfrac{1}{x^2} + 2 = (x - \dfrac{1}{x})^2 + 2 = 3^2 + 2 = 11$.

Problem 34. **Solution:** 3.

$$\frac{x^8+x^7+\cdots+x^2+x+1}{x^6+x^3+1} = \frac{(1-x)(x^8+x^7+\cdots+x^2+x+1)}{(1-x)(x^6+x^3+1)}$$

$$= \frac{1-x^9}{(1-x)(x^6+x^3+1)} = \frac{(1-x^3)(1+x^3+x^6)}{(1-x)(x^6+x^3+1)}$$

$$= \frac{(1-x^3)}{(1-x)} = \frac{(1-x)(1+x+x^2)}{(1-x)} = 1+x+x^2.$$

Thus $1+x+x^2 = 13 \quad \Rightarrow \quad x^2+x-12=0$.

The positive integer value is $x = 3$.

1. BASIC KNOWLEDGE

(1) Consecutive integers with formulas

Sum of consecutive positive integers from 1 to n:

$$1 + 2 + \ldots + n = \frac{1}{2}n(n+1) \qquad (1)$$

Sum of consecutive integers, or sum of consecutive odd/even integers or the sum of a series of integers that have a common difference d.

$$S = na_1 + \frac{n(n-1)d}{2} \qquad \text{(known } a_1, n \text{, and } d\text{)} \qquad (2)$$

$$S = \frac{(a_n - a_1)^2}{2d} + \frac{a_n + a_1}{2} \qquad \text{(known } a_1, a_n \text{, and } d\text{)} \qquad (3)$$

Where a_1 is the beginning number and a_n is the ending number, n is the number of terms, and d is the common difference.

The following formula can be used to compute the sum of consecutive integers that have a common difference.

$$S = m \times n \qquad (4)$$

Where m is the middle number and n is how many numbers in the addition. The middle number is the arithmetic mean of these integers.

Sum of consecutive odd positive integers from 1 to $2n - 1$:

$$1 + 3 + 5 + \ldots + (2n - 1) = n^2 \qquad (5)$$

Sum of consecutive even positive integers from 2 to $2n$:

$$2 + 4 + 6 + \ldots + 2n = n(n+1) \qquad (6)$$

Sum of the squares of consecutive positive integers from 1 to n:

$$1^2 + 2^2 + \ldots + n^2 = \frac{1}{6}n(n+1)(2n+1) \qquad (7)$$

Sum of the cubes of consecutive positive integers from 1 to n:

$$1^3 + 2^3 + \ldots + n^3 = (1 + 2 + \ldots + n)^2 = [\frac{1}{2} n(n+1)]^2 \tag{8}$$

$$(1)(2) + (2)(3) + (3)(4) + \ldots + (n)(n+1) = \frac{n(n+1)(n+2)}{3}$$

$$1 \cdot 2 \cdot 3 + 2 \cdot 3 \cdot 4 + \cdots + n(n+1)(n+2) = \frac{1}{4} n(n+1)(n+2)(n+3).$$

The common difference d

$$d = a_n - a_{n-1} = \frac{a_n - a_1}{n-1} = \frac{a_n - a_m}{n-m} \tag{9}$$

For the list of numbers: 1, 2, 3, 4,…, the common difference is $d = 2 - 1 = 1$.
For the list numbers: 1, 3, 5, 7,…, the common difference $d = 3 - 1 = 2$.
For the list of numbers: 1, 5, 9, 13,…, the common difference is $d = 5 - 1 = 4$.

The number of terms n

$$n = (\text{last term} - \text{first term}) \div d + 1 \tag{10}$$
For consecutive integers: $n = (\text{last term} - \text{first term}) + 1 \tag{11}$

(2). Consecutive integers with partitions

(1). A positive integer N can be written as the sum of consecutive integers only when this positive integer cannot be expressed as a power of 2.

(2). If a positive integer N has n odd factors, then there are $n - 1$ ways to express N as the sum of two or more consecutive positive integers.

(3). There is one way to express any odd prime number as the sum of two or more consecutive positive integers.

(4). For some positive integers m and k,

$$N = m + (m+1) + (m+2) + (m+3) + ... + (m+k-1)$$
$$= \frac{(m+m+k-1)k}{2} = \frac{(2m+k-1)k}{2} \tag{12}$$

(5). $2N = (2m+k-1)k$ \hfill (13)

(7). k and $(2m+k-1)$ have opposite parity, which means that if k is odd, then $(2m+k-1)$ is even and if k is even, then $(2m+k-1)$ is odd.

(8). $(2m+k-1) > k$ \hfill (14)

(9). The greatest number of consecutive integers in a given way of expression.

k_{max} is the greatest number of terms possible:

$$k_{max} \le \left\lfloor \frac{1}{2}(\sqrt{8N+1}-1) \right\rfloor \tag{15}$$

(3) Consecutive integers theorems

Theorem 1: The product of k consecutive integers is divisible by $k!$.

Theorem 2: There must be one positive integer divisible by n among n consecutive positive integers.

Theorem 3: The number of ways to select k non-consecutive elements from n consecutive terms is $N = \dbinom{n-(k-1)}{k}$.

n is the total number of terms. k is the number of elements selected.

2. PROBLEM SOLVING SKILLS

(2. 1) Consecutive integers with formulas

Example 1. What is the sum of all positive odd multiple of 3 that are less than 100?

Solution: 867.
The smallest value is 3 and the greatest value is 99:

$$3 + 9 + 15 + \ldots + 99 = \frac{(3+99)}{2} \times 17 = 867.$$

Example 2. Compute: $37 + 38 + 39 + 40 + 41 + 42 + 43$.

Solution: 280.
$37 + 38 + 39 + 40 + 41 + 42 + 43 = 40 \times 7 = 280.$

Example 3. The sum of five consecutive integers is 2015. What is the greatest of the five integers?

Solution: 405.
The middle number is $2015 / 5 = 13 \times 31 = 403$.
The fourth number is 404 and the fifth number is 405.
Note: $2015 = 5 \times 13 \times 31$.

Example 4. The sum of the pairwise products of three consecutive natural numbers is 1874. What is the largest of the three numbers?

Solution: 26.
Let the three consecutive integers be $(n-1)$, n, $(n+1)$.
We have $(n-1)n + n(n+1) + (n-1)(n+1) = 1874 \qquad \Rightarrow \qquad 3n^2 - 1 = 1874$
$\qquad \Rightarrow \qquad 3n^2 = 1875 \quad \Rightarrow \quad n^2 = 625 \qquad \Rightarrow \qquad n = 25.$
The largest of the three numbers is $n + 1 = 26$.

Example 5. A list consists of 1000 consecutive odd integers. What is the difference between the greatest number in the list and the least number in the list?

Solution: 1998.
Method 1:
Let the first odd integer be $2n + 1$ and the last be $2n + m$.
$2n + m = 2n + 1 + (1000 - 1) \times 2$.
Solving for m we get $m = 1 + 1998 = 1999$.
The answer is $1999 - 1 = 1998$.

Method 2:
Let the 1000 consecutive odd integers be 1, 3, 5,…, x.
$$\frac{x-1}{2} + 1 = 1000 \qquad \Rightarrow \qquad x = 1999.$$
The answer is $1999 - 1 = 1998$.

Example 6. The larger of three consecutive even integers is three times the smaller. What is their sum?

Solution: 12.
Let $2n$ be the smaller term. Then
$(2n + 4) = 3(2n) \qquad \Rightarrow \qquad 4 = 4n \qquad \Rightarrow \qquad n = 1$.
The sum is $(2n) + (2n + 2) + (2n + 4) = 6n + 6 = 12$.

Example 7. The product of three consecutive positive integers is 16 times their sum. What is the sum of their squares?

Solution: 149.
Let the three consecutive integers be $(n - 1)$, n, $(n + 1)$.
We have $(n - 1)n(n + 1) = 16(n - 1 + n + n + 1) \qquad \Rightarrow \qquad (n - 1)n(n + 1) = 16 \times 3n \qquad \Rightarrow \qquad (n - 1)(n + 1) = 48 \qquad \Rightarrow \qquad n^2 - 1 = 48 \qquad \Rightarrow \qquad n^2 = 49$
$n = 7$.
The sum of their squares is $(n - 1)^2 + n^2 + (n + 1)^2 = (7 - 1)^2 + 7^2 + (7 + 1)^2 = 36 + 49 + 64 = 149$.

Example 8. Write the number 105 as the sum of ten consecutive integers. What is the largest one of the ten numbers?

Solution: 15.
We first achieve the middle number: $105 \div 10 = 10.5$. Since 10.5 is not an integer; it is not what we want.

But we can think of 10.5 as one of the ten numbers we want. Then there are 5 numbers to the left of 10.5, where 10 is the nearest number, and 5 numbers to the right of 10.5, where 11 is the nearest one. The five numbers to the right of "10.5" are then 11, 12, 13, 14, and 15. 15 is our answer.

(2. 2) Consecutive integers with patterns

Example 9. (1999 National Sprint problem 30) Squares with sides 1 centimeter long are arranged as shown, each row containing one more square than the row above it. How many centimeters are in the perimeter of the figure formed by arranging 210 squares in this fashion?

Solution: 80.
We first find the pattern of the perimeter of each arrangement as shown below, where n is the number of rows in the figure:

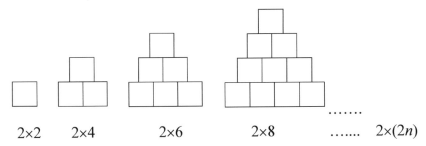

| 2×2 | 2×4 | 2×6 | 2×8 | .... 2×(2n) |

The perimeter of the figure with n rows is equal to $2 \times (2n)$.
Next, we find n in the 20th figure:

$$1+2+3+4+...+n = \frac{(1+n)n}{2} = 210 \qquad \Rightarrow \qquad n = 20.$$

The desired perimeter is $2 \times (2n) = 2 \times 2 \times 20 = 80$.

Example 10. (1997 National Sprint problem 22) The sequence shown was formed by writing the first letter of the alphabet followed by writing the first two letters of the alphabet and continuing the pattern by writing one more letter of the alphabet each time. Continuing this pattern, what letter is the 280th letter in this sequence?

   A, A, B, A, B, C, A, B, C, D, A, B, C, D, E, . . .

Solution: D.

$$1+2+3+4+...+n=\frac{(1+n)n}{2}=280\Rightarrow \qquad (1+n)n=560$$

If $n=23$, then $\dfrac{(1+23)23}{2}=276$.

This means that the 277th term will be A, the 278th term will be B, the 279th term will be C, and the 280th term will be D.

A	B	C	D
277	278	279	280th

Example 11. What is the number that will be listed directly beneath 25 when this triangular array is continued in the same manner?

			1			
		2	3	4		
	5	6	7	8	9	
10	11	12	13	14	15	16

Solution: 35.

Method 1:

Note that the last number in any row is a square number. So we have

10	11	12	13	14	15	16
				25		
			?	36		

35 is the number directly listed below 25.

Method 2:

We know that $1 + 3 + 5 + .. + (2n - 1) = n^2$.

Since $25 = 5^2$, we know that the last number in the 5 row is 25. There are $2n - 1 = 2 \times 5 - 1 = 9$ numbers in the 5th row.

$36 = 6^2$, we know that the last number in the 6 row is 36. There are $2n - 1 = 2 \times 6 - 1 = 11$ numbers in the 6th row.

So there are two more numbers in 6th row. 35 is the number directly listed below 25.

(2. 3) Consecutive integers with partitions

Example 12. If 165 is to be written as the sum of n consecutive positive integers, which of the following cannot be the value of n?

(A) 2   (B) 3   (C) 4   (D) 5   (E) 6

Solution: 4.
We know that $2N = k \times (2m + k - 1)$, where k and $(2m + k - 1)$ have opposite parity, and $(2m + k - 1) > k$.

$2 \times 165 = 2 \times (3 \times 5 \times 11) = 3 \times (2 \times 5 \times 11) = 5 \times (2 \times 3 \times 11) = 6 \times (5 \times 11)$.

So k can be 2, 3, 5, and 6 but cannot be 4.

Example 13. How many ways to write the number 1995 as the sum of two or more consecutive positive integers?

Solution: 15.
$1995 = 5 \times 3 \times 7 \times 19$ has $2 \times 2 \times 2 \times 2 = 16$ odd factors. There are $16 - 1 = 15$ ways to express 1995 as the sum of two or more consecutive positive integers.

Example 14. The sum of n consecutive positive integers is 100. What is the greatest possible value of n?

Solution: 8.
We are seeking for the greatest possible value of k. We know that $k < 2m + k - 1$ and k and $2m + k - 1$ have the different parity, so we set the value for k such that

it is as close as possible to $2m + k - 1$: $2N = k(2m+k-1) = 2^3 \times 5^2 = 5 \times 40 = 8 \times 25$.
So we get $k = 8$.

Example 15. What is the smallest positive integer that can be expressed as the sum of seven consecutive integers, the sum of ten consecutive integers, and the sum of eleven consecutive integers?

Solution: 385.

The sum of seven consecutive integers is 7 times the fourth number. The sum of ten consecutive integers is 5 times the sum of the fifth and the sixth numbers. The sum of eleven consecutive integers is 11 times the sixth number. So the positive integer that can be expressed as the sum of thirteen consecutive integers, the sum of ten consecutive integers, and the sum of eleven consecutive integers must be a multiple of 7, 5, and 11. The smallest such positive integer is $7 \times 5 \times 11 = 385$.

It is easy to check:
385
$= 52 + 53 + 54 + 55 + 56 + 57 + 58$
$= 34 + 35 + 36 + 37 + 38 + 39 + 40 + 41 + 42 + 43$
$= 30 + 31 + 32 + 33 + 34 + 35 + 36 + 37 + 38 + 39 + 40$

Example 16. Find the greatest possible value of k such that 3^{11} can be expressed as the sum of k consecutive positive integers.

Solution: 486.
We know that $2N = k \times (2m+k-1)$, where k and $(2m+k-1)$ have opposite parity, and $(2m+k-1) > k$.
$2 \times 3^{11} = 2 \times 3^5 \times 3^6$.
So the greatest value for k is $2 \times 3^5 = 486$.
The first positive integer is determined: $2m+k-1 = 3^6 = 729 \Rightarrow$

$2m = 3^6 = 729+1-486 = 244 \Rightarrow m = \dfrac{244}{2} = 122$.

The last positive integer is $122 + 486 - 1 = 607$.
So $3^{11} = 122 + 123 + \ldots + 607$.

(2. 4) Formula Applications

Example 17. Find a positive integral solution to the equation
$$\frac{1+3+5+\cdots+(2n-1)}{2+4+6+\cdots+2n} = \frac{2015}{2016}.$$

Solution: 2015.
$$\frac{2015}{2016} = \frac{1+3+5+\cdots+(2n-1)}{2+4+6+\cdots+2n} = \frac{n^2}{n(n+1)} = \frac{n}{n+1};$$
Hence $n = 2015$.

Example 18. Show that for any positive integer n, $n(n+1)(2n+1)$ is always divisible by 6.

Solution:
$$n(n+1)(2n+1) = n(n+1)[(n-1)+(n+2)]$$
$$= (n-1)n(n+1) + n(n+1)(n+2).$$
By Theorem 1, we know that $(n-1)n(n+1)$ is divisible by $3! = 6$ and
$n(n+1)(n+2)$ is also divisible by 6.
Therefore $n(n+1)(2n+1)$ is always divisible by 6.

Example 19. (2015 Mathcounts Handbook 275) Drew purchased a used 50-page book at the book fair. Drew later realized that the book, in which left-hand pages contained even page numbers and right-hand pages contained odd page numbers, did not contain all 50 pages. The sum of the page numbers on the pages that Drew's book did contain was 1242. What is the greatest page number that could be on a page missing from Drew's book?

Solution: 12.

If no page was missing we have the sum $1 + 2 + \cdots + 50 = \dfrac{50(50+1)}{2} = 1275$.

$1275 - 1242 = 33$. So the sum of the page numbers missing is 33.
If only one page was missing, we have $16 + 17 = 33$. But the right-hand page contains the odd page number. 16 is not an odd number.

So we assume that 2 pages were missing.
We have $(2n + 1 + 2n + 2) + (2m + 1 + 2m + 2) = 33$.
n and m are nonnegative integers.

This is not possible because the left-hand side is even and the right-hand is odd.

Then we assume that 3 pages were missing.
We have $(2n + 1 + 2n + 2) + (2m + 1 + 2m + 2) + (2p + 1 + 2p + 2) = 33$
n, m and p are nonnegative integers.
The above equation can be simplified as $4n + 4m + 4p + 9 = 33$
$\Rightarrow 4n + 4m + 4p = 24 \Rightarrow n + m + p = 6$.
Since we want the greatest page number in one page, we let $n = 0$, $m = 1$ to get $p = 5$. The greatest page number is $2p + 2 = 12$.

Example 20. The pages of a book are numbered 1 through n. When the page numbers of the book were added, one of the page numbers was mistakenly added twice, resulting in an incorrect sum of 2014. What was the number of the page that was added twice?

Solution: 61.
Let k be the page number added twice. $0 < k < n + 1$.

$1 + 2 + \ldots + n < 1 + 2 + \ldots + n + k < 1 + 2 + \ldots + n + (n + 1)$, or
$$\frac{n(n+1)}{2} < 2014 < \frac{(n+1)(n+2)}{2} \qquad \Rightarrow \qquad n(n+1) < 4020 < (n+1)(n+2)$$
We know that $62 \times 63 = 3906$ and $63 \times 64 = 4032$. So $n = 62$.
$k = 2014 - \dfrac{62 \times 63}{2} = 61$.

Example 21. It is known that, for all positive integers k,

$1^2 + 2^2 + 3^2 + \cdots + k^2 = \dfrac{k(k+1)(2k+1)}{6}$. Find the smallest positive integer k such

that $1^2 + 2^2 + 3^2 + \cdots + k^2$ is a multiple of 100.

Solution: 24.
The sum is a multiple of 100 if and only if $k(k+1)(2k+1) = 6 \times 100N = 2^3 \times 3 \times 5N$ for some positive integer N. Because $2k+1$ is odd and k and $k+1$ cannot both be even, it follows that either k or $k+1$ is a multiple of 8 (we have taken care of 2^3 in the factors $2^3 \times 3 \times 5N$). Furthermore, the product is divisible by 6 then divisible by 3 for all integer values of k (we have taken care of 3 in the factors $2^3 \times 3 \times 5N$). $k = 8, 9, 16, 17, 24, 25, \ldots$ We see that when $k = 24$, $k(k+1)(2k+1)$ is divisible by 25 (we have taken care of 5^2 in the factors $2^3 \times 3 \times 5N$). So 24 is the smallest positive integer for which $k(k+1)(2k+1)$ is a multiple of 100.

Example 22. Suppose that n is the product of three consecutive integers and that n is divisible by 11. Which of the following is not necessarily a divisor of n?
  (A) 6   (B) 11   (C) 22   (D) 36   (E) 66

Solution: D.
Whenever n is the product of three consecutive integers, n is divisible by 3!, meaning it is divisible by 6. It also mentions that it is divisible by 11, so the number is definitely divisible by all the factors of 66.

In our answer choices, the one that is not a factor of 66 is D.

(2. 5) Consecutive integers with restrictions

Example 23. Alex wants to select two different numbers from {2, 3, 4, 5, 6, 7, 8, 9}. How many ways are there to do so such that these two numbers are not consecutive?

Solution: 21.
Method 1 (Listing):

Case I:

First integer: 2
Second integer: 4, 5, 6, 7, 8, or 9
6 ways.

Case II:
First integer: 3
Second integer: 5, 6, 7, 8, or 9
5 ways.

Case III:
First integer: 4
Second integer: 6, 7, 8, or 9
4 ways.

Case IV:
First integer: 5
Second integer: 7, 8, or 9
3 ways.

Case V:
First integer: 6
Second integer: 8 or 9
2 ways.

Case VI:
First integer: 7
Second integer: 9
1 way.

Total $6 + 5 + 4 + 3 + 2 + 1 = 21$ ways.

Method 2:
The number of ways to select k non-consecutive elements from n consecutive terms is $N = \dbinom{n - (k-1)}{k}$.

n is the total number of terms.
k is the number of elements selected.

$n = 9 - 2 + 1 = 8. \ k = 2.$

$$N = \binom{n-(k-1)}{k} = \binom{8-(2-1)}{k} = \binom{7}{2} = 21.$$

Example 24. (2006 AMC Problem 25) How many non-empty subsets S of {1, 2, 3,..., 15} have the following two properties?
(1) No two consecutive integers belong to S.
(2) If S contains k elements, then S contains no number less than k.
(A) 277   (B) 311   (C) 376   (D) 377   (E) 405

Solution: (E).
(our solution) The number of ways to select k non-consecutive elements from n consecutive terms is $N = \binom{n-(k-1)}{k}$.

If $k = 1$, $n = 15$, then $N_1 = \binom{15}{1} = 15$.

If $k = 2$, $n = 14$ (S contains no number less than 2), then $N_2 = \binom{13}{2} = 78$.

If $k = 3$, $n = 13$, (S contains no number less than 3) then $N_3 = \binom{11}{3} = 165$.

If $k = 4$, $n = 12$, (S contains no number less than 4) then $N_4 = \binom{9}{4} = 126$.

If $k = 5$, $n = 11$, then $N_5 = \binom{7}{5} = 21$.

If $k = 6$, $n = 10$, then $N_6 = \binom{5}{6}$ (not possible).

Total: $15 + 78 + 165 + 126 + 21 = 405$.
Note: this was the last problem of the test.

Example 25. The sum of 15 consecutive positive integers is a perfect square. Find the smallest possible value of this sum.

Solution: 225.

$$N = m + (m+1) + (m+2) + (m+3) + ... + (m+k-1)$$

$$= \frac{(m+m+k-1)k}{2} = \frac{(2m+k-1)k}{2}$$

$$= \frac{(2m+14)15}{2} = 15m + 105 = 15(m+7)$$

Since we want the smallest sum, we let $m = 8$.

The answer is 225.

3.PROBLEMS

Problem 1. How many terms are there in the sequence $11 + 12 + 13 + .. + 100$?

Problem 2. How many terms are there in the sequence $2 + 4 + 6 + .. + 100$?

Problem 3. Compute: $38 + 39 + 40 + 41 + 42 + 43$.

Problem 4. The sum of six consecutive positive integers is 2019. What is the largest of these six integers?

Problem 5. The sum of twenty five consecutive integers is 3875. What is the smallest of these integers?

Problem 6. (Mathcounts) Suppose the numbers 1, 2, 3,… are written in a pyramid as shown. In what row does the number 100 appear?

$$1$$
$$2 \quad 3$$
$$4 \quad 5 \quad 6$$
$$7 \quad 8 \quad 9 \quad 10$$
$$\ldots$$

Problem 7. (Mathcounts) When the positive integers are written in the triangular form shown, in what row does the number 1994 appear?

```
1
2   3   4
5   6   7   8   9
10    ...
```

Problem 8. What is the numeral that will be listed directly beneath 25 when this triangular array is continued in the same manner?

```
1
2    3
4    5    6
7    8    9    10
11   12   13   14   15
```

Problem 9. Find the number of sets of two or more consecutive positive integers whose sum is 100.

Problem 10. 1000 students are arranged in several rows (more than 16). The numbers of students in each row are consecutive positive integers. How many students are there in the first row?

Problem 11. The number 585 can be written as the sum of two consecutive integers, 292 and 293. What is the greatest number of consecutive positive integers whose sum is 585?

Problem 12. How many ways to write the number 2009 as the sum of two or more consecutive positive integers?

Problem 13. The number 210 can be written as the sum of consecutive positive integers in several ways. When written as the sum of the greatest possible number of consecutive positive integers, what is the largest of these integers?

Problem 14. Express 84 as the sum of k different positive integers. What is the greatest possible value of k?

Problem 15. The pages of a book are numbered 1 through n. When the page numbers of the book were added, one of the page numbers was mistakenly added twice, resulting in the incorrect sum of 1986. What was the number of the page that was added twice?

Problem 16. If $S_n = 1 + 2 + 3 + \ldots + n$, n is natural number. Find the greatest value of $f(n) = \dfrac{S_n}{(n+32)S_{n+1}}$.

Problem 17. (NC Math League) The sum of the squares of the first N natural number is given by the formula $S_N = \dfrac{N(N+1)(2N+1)}{6}$. Find the sum of the first 50 terms of series $(1)(2) + (2)(3) + (3)(4) + \ldots + (N)(N+1)$.

Problem 18. (AMC) If n is any whole number, $n^2(n^2 - 1)$ is always divisible by:
(A) 12   (B) 24   (C) any multiple of 12   (D) $12 - n$ (E) 12 and 24

Problem 19. Show that the sum of 1 and the product of any four consecutive positive integers is a square number.

Problem 20. Calculate the value of $\sqrt{(25)(24)(23)(22) + 1}$

Problem 21. If the sum $1+2+3+4+...+n$ is a perfect square N^2 and if N is less than 10, how many possible value for n?

Problem 22. (Bulgarian Mathematical Olympiad) Find the number of ways of choosing 6 among the first 49 positive integers, at least two of which are consecutive.

Problem 23. Alex wants to select three different numbers from {2, 3, 4, 5, 6, 7, 8, 9, 10, 11, 12, 13, 14, 15}. How many ways are there such that no two numbers are consecutive?

Problem 24. Alex wants to select four different numbers from {2, 3, 4, 5, 6, 7, 8, 9, 10, 11, 12, 13, 14, 15}. How many ways are there such that no two numbers are consecutive?

4. SOLUTIONS

Problem 1. Solution: 90.
$n = 100 - 11 + 1 = 90$.

Problem 2. Solution: 50.
$n = (100 - 2)/2 + 1 = 50$.

Problem 3. Solution: 243.

$$38 + 39 + 40 + 41 + 42 + 43 = (\frac{40+41}{2}) \times 6 = 81 \times 3 = 243$$

Problem 4. Solution: 339.
The average of the six integers is $2019/6 = 336.5$, so $2019 = 334 + 335 + 336 + 337 + 338 + 339$. The largest of the six integers is 339.

Problem 5. Solution: 143.
The thirteenth number is the average value, or $a_{13} = 3875/25 = 155$.
The smallest of these integers is $155 - 12 = 143$.

Problem 6. Solution: 14.

$$1 + 2 + 3 + ... + n = \frac{n(n+1)}{2}.$$

We know that $\frac{13(13+1)}{2} = 91 < 100 < \frac{14(14+1)}{2} = 105$.

So 100 is in $n = 14^{\text{th}}$ row.

Problem 7. Solution: 45.
We know that $1 + 3 + 5 + ... + (2n - 1) = n^2$.
Since $1936 = 44^2 < 1994 < 45^2 = 2025$, we know that the first number in the 45 row is 1937 and the last number in the 45 row is 2025.

Problem 8. Solution: 32.

$$1+2+3+...+n = \frac{n(n+1)}{2}.$$

There are 7 numbers in the 7th row. 25 is in the 7th row since the last number in the 7th row is $\frac{7(7+1)}{2} = 28$. We count backward four times to 25: 28, 27, 26, 25.

There are 8 numbers in the 8th row. The last number in the 8th row is $\frac{8(8+1)}{2} = 36$. We count backward five times: 36, 35, 34, 33, 32.

So 32 is the number beneath 25.

Problem 9. Solution: 2.
$100 = 2^2 \times 5^2$. The number of odd factors of 100 is 3. The solution will be 3 – 1 = 2.

Problem 10. Solution: 28.
Let m be the number of students in the first row.
$m+(m+1)+(m+2)+.....+(m+k-1)=1000$
$(2m+k-1)\times k = 1000\times 2 = 2^4 \times 5^3$.
We know that $k > 16$, and $2m + k - 1$ and k must have different parity, so we can only have $(2m+k-1)\times k = 1000\times 2 = 2^4 \times 5^3 = 25\times 80$
So $k = 25$ and $2m + k - 1 = 80$ $\Rightarrow$ $m = 28$.

Problem 11. Solution: 30.
Method 1:
If a sum of consecutive positive integers starts with a number greater than 1, then we can think of this sum as the difference between two triangular numbers. The number 595 is the 34th triangular number, and it is 10 more than our number 585. Ten is the fourth triangular number, so this sum must consist of $34 - 4 = 30$ consecutive positive integers.

Method 2:
$(2m+k-1)\times k = 2N$
We need to write $2N$ as the product of two integers that are as close as possible in order to obtain the greatest number.

$2N = 2 \times 585 = 1170 = 2 \times 3^2 \times 5 \times 13 = 30 \times 39$
Since k is the smaller value of the two factors, $k = 30$.

Problem 12. Solution: 5.
2009 has 6 odd factors. $6 - 1 = 5$. There are 5 ways to write 2009 as the sum of two or more consecutive positive integers.

Problem 13. Solution: 20.
We have: $2N = (2m + k - 1)k$ or $k(2m + k - 1) = 2 \times 2 \times 5 \times 3 \times 7$
We are looking for the greatest possible value of k. We know that $k < 2m + k - 1$ and that k and $2m + k - 1$ have different parity, so we set the value for k so that it is as close as possible to $2m + k - 1$: $k(2m + k - 1) = 20 \times 21$.
$k = 20$ and $2m + k - 1 = 21$. We get $k = 20$ and $m = 1$.
The value of the greatest term $= m + k - 1 = 1 + 20 - 1 = 20$.

Problem 14. Solution: 8.
We know: $m + (m + 1) + (m + 2) + \ldots + (m + k - 1) = N$, or

$2N = (2m + k - 1) \times k$.

$(2m + k - 1) \times k = 2 \times 84 = 2^3 \times 3 \times 7$
We know that $k < 2m + k - 1$ and that k and $2m + k - 1$ have different parity, so we set the value for k so that it is as close as possible to $2m + k - 1$:
$k(2m + k - 1) = 8 \times 21$.
So $k = 8$.
Note that $2m + k - 1 = 21$ and $m = 7$. $84 = 7 + 8 + 9 + 10 + 11 + 12 + 13 + 14$.

Problem 15. Solution: 33.
We calculate the possible k values first by using the formula:

$k = \left\lfloor \frac{1}{2}(\sqrt{8 \times 1986 + 1} - 1) \right\rfloor = \lfloor 62.5 \rfloor = 62$.

And then we calculate the correct sum of the numbers:

$N = \frac{(1 + 62) \times 62}{2} = 1953$.

Finally, we know that the number that was mistakenly added twice is $1986 - 1953 = 33$.

Problem 16. Solution: $\dfrac{1}{50}$.

By the formula of the sum of the first n terms of an arithmetic

sequence: $S_n = \dfrac{1}{2}n(n+1)$, $S_{n+1} = \dfrac{1}{2}(n+1)(n+2)$

We have $f(n) = \dfrac{S_n}{(n+32)S_{n+1}} = \dfrac{n}{n^2+34n+64} = \dfrac{1}{n+34+\dfrac{64}{n}} = $

$\dfrac{1}{(\sqrt{n}-\dfrac{8}{\sqrt{n}})^2+50} \le \dfrac{1}{50}$

So when $\sqrt{n} - \dfrac{8}{\sqrt{8}}$, or $n = 8$, $f(n)_{max} = \dfrac{1}{50}$.

Problem 17. Solution: 44,200.

Each term of the given series is in the form $N(N+1)$, which may be rewritten as $N^2 + N$. We are given that $1^2 + 2^2 + 3^2 + \cdots + N^2 = \dfrac{N(N+1)(2N+1)}{6}$. We also can

show that $1 + 2 + 3 + \cdots + N = \dfrac{N(N+1)}{2}$. Now we have

$(1+1^2)+(2+2^2)+(3+3^2)+\cdots+(N+N^2) = \dfrac{N(N+1)(2N+1)}{6} + \dfrac{N(N+1)}{2}$. Thus

the given series has a sum of $\dfrac{N(N+1)(2N+4)}{6}$ or $\dfrac{N(N+1)(N+2)}{3}$. Thus if $N =$

50, the sum is $\dfrac{(50)(51)(52)}{3}$ or 44,200.

Problem 18. Solution: A.

Method 1 (official solution):

By considering the special case $n = 2$, $n^2(n^2 - 1) = 12$, we can immediately rule out choices (B), (C), (D), and (E), leaving us the answer (A). This is an immediate way to get the answer.

Method 2 (official solution):
$n^2(n^2 - 1) = n\{(n - 1)n(n + 1)\} = nk$, where k is a product of three consecutive integers, $n - 1$, n, and $n + 1$, hence always divisible by 3.
Since n is a factor of k, if n is even, k is also divisible by 2 and hence by 6. Thus, nk will be divisible by 12.
If n is odd, since the even numbers $n - 1$ and $n + 1$ are factors of k, k is divisible also by 4 and hence by 12. Thus, nk will be divisible by 12.

Method 3 (our solution):
$n^2(n^2 - 1) = n(n - 1)n(n + 1)$.
If n is even, then by **Theorem 1**, $(n - 1)n(n + 1)$ is always divisible by $3! = 6$, and so
$n(n - 1)n(n + 1)$ is divisible by 12.
If n is odd, then by **Theorem 2**, one of the positive integers $(n - 1)$, n, and $(n + 1)$ is divisible by 3. Since n is odd, both $(n - 1)$ and $(n + 1)$ are even, and so $(n - 1)(n + 1)$ is divisible by 4.
Thus, $n(n - 1)n(n + 1)$ is divisible by 12.

Problem 19. Solution:
Let n be the first positive integer.
The product of the four consecutive integers is then
$n(n + 1)(n + 2)(n + 3) + 1$
$= (n^2 + 3n)(n^2 + 3n + 2) + 1$
$= (n^2 + 3n + 1 - 1)(n^2 + 3n + 1 + 1) +$
$= (n^2 + 3n + 1)^2 - 1 + 1 = (n^2 + 3n + 1)^2$

Problem 20. Solution: 551.
We know that $x(x+1)(x+2)(x+3) + 1 = (x^2 + 3x + 1)^2$.

Let $x = 22$, $\sqrt{(25)(24)(23)(22)+1} = (22^2 + 3 \times 22 + 1) = 551$.

Problem 21. Solution: 2.

$$S = 1 + 2 + 3 + 4 + \ldots + n = \frac{(1+n)n}{2} = N^2 \qquad \Rightarrow \qquad n^2 + n - 2N^2 = 0$$

The possible values for N^2 are $1^2, 2^2, \ldots, 10^2$.

Since n is a positive integer, we have $\Delta = m^2 \qquad \Rightarrow \qquad 1 + 8N^2 = m^2 \Rightarrow$

The possible values for N^2 are reduced to 1, and 6^2. The values for n are 1 and 8.

Problem 22. Solution: $\dbinom{49}{6} - \dbinom{44}{6}$.

There are $\dbinom{49}{6}$ ways to select 6 numbers among the first 49 positive integers.

There are $\dbinom{n-(k-1)}{k} = \dbinom{44}{6}$ ways to select 6 numbers among the first 49

positive integers such that no two of which are consecutive.

The number of ways of choosing 6 among the first 49 positive integers, where at least two of which are consecutive, is $\dbinom{49}{6} - \dbinom{44}{6}$.

Problem 23. Solution: 220.

$$N = \dbinom{n-(k-1)}{k} = \dbinom{14-(3-1)}{3} = \dbinom{12}{3} = 220.$$

Problem 24. Solution: 330.

$$N = \dbinom{n-(k-1)}{k} = \dbinom{14-(4-1)}{4} = \dbinom{11}{4} = 330.$$

BASIC KNOWLEDGE

(1). Definitions

Sets: A set is any well-defined collection of objects. Individual objects are called the elements or members of the set.

Subsets: A subset is a sub-collection of a set. We denote set B as subset of A by the notation $B \subseteq A$.

Proper subset: If B is a subset of A and B is not equal to A, B is a proper subset of A, written as $B \subset A$.

Universal set: denoted by U, is the set that contains all elements considered in a given discussion.

(2). The complement of a set

The complement of A, written as $\overline{A}$, represented by the shaded region in the figure below, is the set of all elements in the universal set U that are not in A. The key word in the definition of complement is not.

(3) Intersection of Sets

The intersection of sets A and B, written as $A \cap B$, is the set of all elements belonging to both A and B.

$A \cap B \Rightarrow A$ and B

* One simple way to remember this:

note $\cap$ is like the second letter in the word "and."

$A \cap B$

(4) Union of sets

The union of sets A and B, written as $A \cup B$, is the set of all elements belonging to either A or B.

*Note that the symbol $\cup$ is like the first letter in the word "Union".

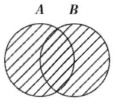

$A \cup B$

(5) Three important formulas

Two Events Union Formula
$$n(A \cup B) = n(A) + n(B) - n(A \cap B)$$

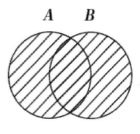

$A \cup B$

Three Events Union Formula
The union of sets A, B, and C, written as $A \cup B \cup C$, is the set of all elements belonging to A, or B, or C.
$$n(A \cup B \cup C) = n(A) + n(B) + n(C)$$
$$- n(A \cap B) - n(B \cap C) - n(C \cap A) + n(A \cap B \cap C)$$

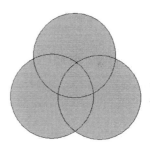

Four Events Formula
The union of A, B, C, and D can be found by:
$$n(A \cup B \cup C \cup D) = n(A) + n(B) + n(C) + n(D)$$
$$- n(A \cap B) - n(A \cap C) - n(A \cap D) - n(B \cap C) - n(B \cap D) - n(C \cap D)$$
$$+ n(A \cap B \cap C) + n(A \cap B \cap D) + n(A \cap C \cap D) + n(B \cap C \cap D)$$
$$- n(A \cap B \cap C \cap D).$$

PROBLEM SOLVING SKILLS

Problems involving "divisible"

Example 1. How many positive integers among 1 and 300 inclusive that are multiples of 3?

Solution: 100.

$$\left\lfloor \frac{300}{3} \right\rfloor = 100$$

Example 2. How many positive integers among 1 and 300 inclusive that are multiples of 4?

Solution: 75.

$$\left\lfloor \frac{300}{4} \right\rfloor = 75$$

Example 3. How many positive integers among 1 and 300 inclusive that are multiples of 5?

Solution: 60.

$$\left\lfloor \frac{300}{5} \right\rfloor = 60$$

Example 4. How many positive integers among 1 and 300 inclusive that are multiples of 3 and 4?

Solution: 25.

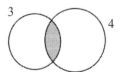

$$\left\lfloor \frac{300}{3 \times 4} \right\rfloor = 25$$

Example 5. How many positive integers among 1 and 300 inclusive that are multiples of 4 and 5?

Solution: 15.

$$\left\lfloor \frac{300}{4 \times 5} \right\rfloor = 15$$

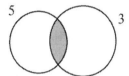

Example 6. How many positive integers among 1 and 300 inclusive that are multiples of 3 and 5?

Solution: 20.

$$\left\lfloor \frac{300}{3 \times 5} \right\rfloor = 20$$

Example 7. How many positive integers among 1 and 300 inclusive that are multiples of 3 and 4 and 5?

Solution: 5.

$$\left\lfloor \frac{300}{3 \times 4 \times 5} \right\rfloor = 5$$

Example 8. How many positive integers among 1 and 300 inclusive that are multiples of 3 or 4?

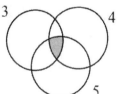

Solution: 150.

$$n(A \cup B) = n(A) + n(B) - n(A \cap B)$$

$$\left\lfloor \frac{300}{3} \right\rfloor + \left\lfloor \frac{300}{4} \right\rfloor - \left\lfloor \frac{300}{3 \times 4} \right\rfloor = 100 + 75 - 25 = 150$$

Example 9. How many positive integers among 1 and 300 inclusive that are multiples of 3 or 5?

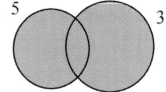

Solution: 140.

$$\left\lfloor \frac{300}{3} \right\rfloor + \left\lfloor \frac{300}{5} \right\rfloor - \left\lfloor \frac{300}{3 \times 5} \right\rfloor = 100 + 60 - 20 = 140$$

Example 10. How many positive integers among 1 and 300 inclusive that are multiples of 4 or 5?

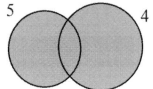

$$\left\lfloor \frac{300}{4} \right\rfloor + \left\lfloor \frac{300}{5} \right\rfloor - \left\lfloor \frac{300}{4 \times 5} \right\rfloor = 75 + 60 - 15 = 120$$

Example 11. How many positive integers among 1 and 300 inclusive that are multiples of 3, 4 or 5?

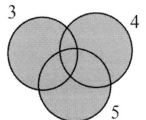

Solution: 180.

$$n(A \cup B \cup C) = n(A) + n(B) + n(C)$$
$$- n(A \cap B) - n(B \cap C) - n(C \cap A) + n(A \cap B \cap C)$$

$100 + 75 + 60 - (25 + 15 + 20) + 5 = 180.$

Example 12. How many positive integers among 1 and 300 inclusive that are multiples of 3, or 4 but not 5?

Solution: 120.

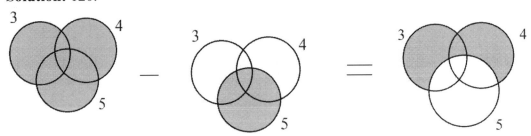

$$\left\lfloor \frac{300}{3} \right\rfloor + \left\lfloor \frac{300}{4} \right\rfloor + \left\lfloor \frac{300}{5} \right\rfloor - \left\lfloor \frac{300}{3 \times 4} \right\rfloor - \left\lfloor \frac{300}{3 \times 5} \right\rfloor - \left\lfloor \frac{300}{4 \times 5} \right\rfloor + \left\lfloor \frac{300}{3 \times 4 \times 5} \right\rfloor$$
$$= 100 + 75 + 60 - 25 - 20 - 15 + 5 = 180$$

$$\left\lfloor \frac{300}{5} \right\rfloor = 60.$$

So the answer is $180 - 60 = 120$.

Example 13. How many positive integers among 1 and 300 inclusive that are multiples of 3, or 5 but not 4?

Solution: 105.

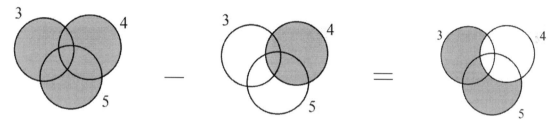

$$\left\lfloor \frac{300}{3} \right\rfloor + \left\lfloor \frac{300}{4} \right\rfloor + \left\lfloor \frac{300}{5} \right\rfloor - \left\lfloor \frac{300}{3 \times 4} \right\rfloor - \left\lfloor \frac{300}{3 \times 5} \right\rfloor - \left\lfloor \frac{300}{4 \times 5} \right\rfloor + \left\lfloor \frac{300}{3 \times 4 \times 5} \right\rfloor$$
$$= 100 + 75 + 60 - 25 - 20 - 15 + 5 = 180$$

$$\left\lfloor \frac{300}{4} \right\rfloor = 75.$$

So the answer is $180 - 75 = 105$.

Example 14. How many positive integers among 1 and 300 inclusive that are multiples of 4, 5 but not 3?

Solution: 80.

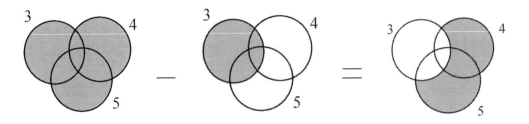

$$\left\lfloor\frac{300}{3}\right\rfloor+\left\lfloor\frac{300}{4}\right\rfloor+\left\lfloor\frac{300}{5}\right\rfloor-\left\lfloor\frac{300}{3\times4}\right\rfloor-\left\lfloor\frac{300}{3\times5}\right\rfloor-\left\lfloor\frac{300}{4\times5}\right\rfloor+\left\lfloor\frac{300}{3\times4\times5}\right\rfloor$$
$$=100+75+60-25-20-15+5=180$$

$$\left\lfloor\frac{300}{3}\right\rfloor=100.$$

So the answer is $180 - 100 = 80$.

Example 15. A positive integer is randomly selected from all positive integers among 1 and 300 inclusive that are multiples of 3, 4, or 5. What is the probability that the positive integer selected is not divisible by 5? Express your answer as a common fraction.

Solution: $\dfrac{2}{3}$

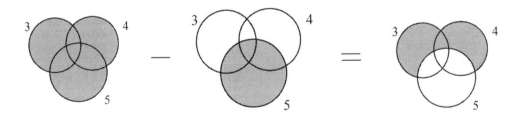

$$\left\lfloor\frac{300}{3}\right\rfloor+\left\lfloor\frac{300}{4}\right\rfloor+\left\lfloor\frac{300}{5}\right\rfloor-\left\lfloor\frac{300}{3\times4}\right\rfloor-\left\lfloor\frac{300}{3\times5}\right\rfloor-\left\lfloor\frac{300}{4\times5}\right\rfloor+\left\lfloor\frac{300}{3\times4\times5}\right\rfloor$$
$$=100+75+60-25-20-15+5=180$$

$$\left\lfloor\frac{300}{5}\right\rfloor=60$$

$$180-60=120.$$

The probability is $P=\dfrac{120}{180}=\dfrac{2}{3}$.

Example 16. A positive integer is randomly selected from all positive integers among 1 and 300 inclusive that are multiples of 3, 4, or 5. What is the probability that the positive integer selected is divisible by 5 only? Express your answer as a common fraction.

Solution: $\dfrac{1}{6}$.

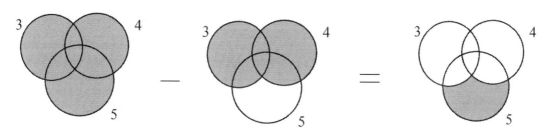

$$\left\lfloor\frac{300}{3}\right\rfloor+\left\lfloor\frac{300}{4}\right\rfloor+\left\lfloor\frac{300}{5}\right\rfloor-\left\lfloor\frac{300}{3\times4}\right\rfloor-\left\lfloor\frac{300}{3\times5}\right\rfloor-\left\lfloor\frac{300}{4\times5}\right\rfloor+\left\lfloor\frac{300}{3\times4\times5}\right\rfloor$$
$$=100+75+60-25-20-15+5=180$$

$$\left\lfloor\frac{300}{3}\right\rfloor+\left\lfloor\frac{300}{4}\right\rfloor-\left\lfloor\frac{300}{3\times4}\right\rfloor=100+75-25=150$$

$180 - 150 = 30$.

The probability is $P = \dfrac{30}{180} = \dfrac{1}{6}$.

Example 17. How many positive integers not exceeding 300 are multiples of 3 or 4 but not 15?

Solution: 130.

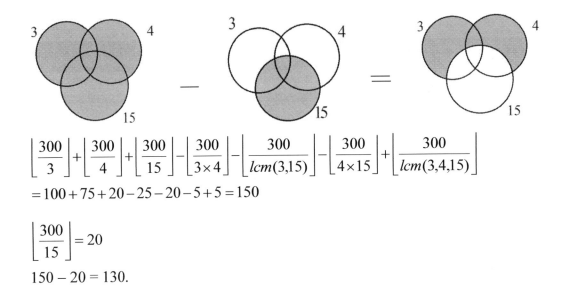

$$\left\lfloor \frac{300}{3} \right\rfloor + \left\lfloor \frac{300}{4} \right\rfloor + \left\lfloor \frac{300}{15} \right\rfloor - \left\lfloor \frac{300}{3 \times 4} \right\rfloor - \left\lfloor \frac{300}{lcm(3,15)} \right\rfloor - \left\lfloor \frac{300}{4 \times 15} \right\rfloor + \left\lfloor \frac{300}{lcm(3,4,15)} \right\rfloor$$

$= 100 + 75 + 20 - 25 - 20 - 5 + 5 = 150$

$$\left\lfloor \frac{300}{15} \right\rfloor = 20$$

$150 - 20 = 130$.

Problems involving " like" and "dislike"

Example 18: (Mathcounts Competitions) In a class of 500 students, every student liked at least one for three kinds of music.
260 liked classical music
260 liked jazz music
 75 liked classical and rock music
115 liked rock and jazz music
130 liked classical and jazz music

45 liked classical, jazz, and rock music

How many of the students in this class liked only rock music?

Solution: 110 (students).

Set A: number of students who liked classical music (260).

Set B: number of students who liked jazz music (260).

Set C: number of students who liked rock music (x).

Method 1:

The union of sets A, B, and C is:

$n(A \cup B \cup C) = n(A) + n(B) + n(C)$

$- n(A \cap B) - n(B \cap C) - n(C \cap A) + n(A \cap B \cap C)$

Substituting all constants into the formula:

$500 = 260 + 260 + x - (75 + 115 + 130) + 45 \qquad \Rightarrow \qquad x = 255$

We are able to draw the following Venn diagrams:

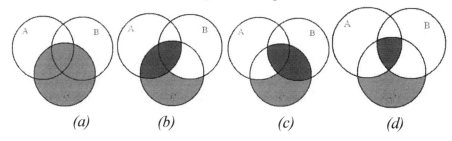

(a)   (b)   (c)   (d)

The answer is $(a) - (b) - (c) + (d) = 255 - 75 - 115 + 45 = 110$.

Method 2:

The solution will be $n(A \cup B \cup C) - n(A \cup B)$.

$n(A \cup B \cup C) = 500$ and $n(A \cup B) = 260 + 260 - 130 = 390$.

The answer is $500 - 390 = 110$.

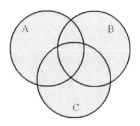 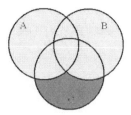

Example 19: (Mathcounts Competitions) Of the 400 eighth-graders at Pascal Middle school, 117 take algebra, 109 take advanced computer, 114 take industrial technology. Furthermore, 70 take both algebra and advanced computer, 34 take both algebra and industrial technology, and 29 take both advanced computer and industrial technology. Finally, 164 students take none of these courses. How many students take all three courses?

Solution: 29 (students).

We are given:

Set A: number of students taking Algebra (117).

Set B: number of students taking advanced computer (109).

Set C: number of students taking industrial technology (109).

 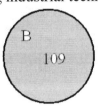 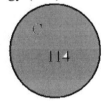

We also know that $n(A \cap B) = 70$, $n(A \cap C) = 34$, and $n(B \cap C) = 29$.

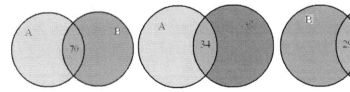

We like to find the number of students who are taking three subjects.

This is the same as finding $n(A \cap B \cap C)$, the intersection of sets A, B and C.

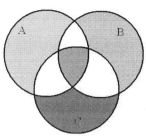

We first need to find the total number of students who participated in the events:
$n(A \cup B \cup C) = 400 - 164 = 236$

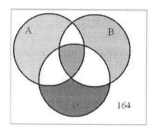

By the formula:
$236 = 117 + 109 + 114 - 70 - 34 - 29 + n(A \cap B \cap C) \implies$
$n(A \cap B \cap C) = 236 - 207 = 29$

Example 20: Out of 22 students surveyed on ice cream flavors, 12 like chocolate, 5 like only strawberry, and 6 liked vanilla. If 3 liked chocolate and vanilla, how many students did not like any of these flavors?

Solution: 2 (students)
We are given:
Set A: number of students favoring chocolate (12), Set C: number of students favoring vanilla (6), and the intersection of sets A and C (3). The universal set $U = 22$.

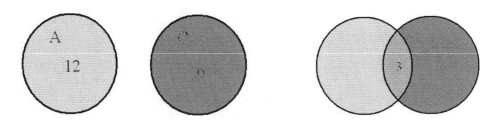

From $n(A \cup C) = n(A) + n(C) - n(A \cap C)$ $\Rightarrow$ $n(A \cup C) = 12 + 6 - 3 = 15$.

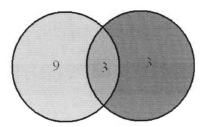

We are also given the number of students favoring only strawberry (5).

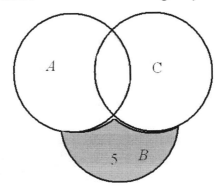

The union of A B, and C can be found this way:
$n(A \cup B \cup C) = 15 + 5 = 20$.

We want to find x, the number of students who did not like any of these flavors:
$x = 22 - n(A \cup B \cup C)$.

The answer is $22 - 20 = 2$.

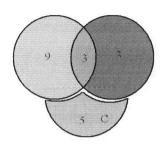

Example 21. (1998 Mathcounts State Sprint) Every camper at camp EKO is required to take exactly two of the three crafts classes offered. One summer, 47 campers took basket weaving, 59 took cabinet making, and 34 took pottery. How many campers attended camp EKO that summer?

Solution: 70 (campers).
The total number of classes at camp EKO is 47 + 59 + 34 = 140. Since each person takes exactly two classes, the number of campers is 140 ÷ 2 = 70.

Example 22. There are 100 5th graders in Hope Middle School. 58 like English, 38 like Math, and 52 like Spanish. 6 students like Math and English only (not Spanish), 4 students like Math and Spanish only (not English), and 12 students like all three subjects. Each student likes at least one subject. How many students only like English?

Solution: 26.
Let x be the number of students who like English and Spanish (but not Math).
By the formula: $n(A \cup B \cup C) = n(A) + n(B) + n(C)$
$- n(A \cap B) - n(B \cap C) - n(C \cap A) + n(A \cap B \cap C)$

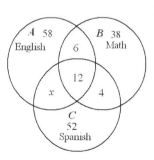

$100 = 58 + 52 + 38 - (6 + 12 + 12 + x + 12 + 4) + 12$
$\Rightarrow \quad x = 14.$
The answer is $58 - 6 - 12 - 14 = 26.$
The Venn diagram is shown on the right:

Problems involving "at least" or "at most"

Example 23. 8th grade classes are surveyed. 78% of the students like swimming, 80% like computer games, 84% like playing chess and 88% like reading books. At least how many percent of students like all four activities?

Solution: 30%.
Let the number of students be 100.
Number of students does not like swimming: $100 - 78 = 22$.
Number of students does not like computer games: $100 - 80 = 20$.
Number of students does not like playing chess: $100 - 84 = 16$.
Number of students does not like reading books: $100 - 88 = 12$.
At most, the number of students does not like at least one of the three activities is:

$22 + 20 + 16 + 12 = 70$.
At least $100 - 70 = 30$ or 30 percent of students like all four activities.

Example 24. There are 52 students in a class. 30 of them can swim. 35 can ride bicycle. 42 can play table tennis. At least how many students can do all three sports?

Solution: 3.
Method 1: Number of students who cannot swim: $52 - 30 = 22$.
Number of students who cannot ride bicycle: $52 - 35 = 17$.
Number of students who cannot play tennis: $52 - 42 = 10$.
At most $22 + 17 + 10 = 49$ students cannot play at least one of the three activities.
At least $52 - 49 = 3$ students can do all three sports.

Method 2: **The tickets method**
Step 1: Give each student a ticket for each activity he or she likes. $30 + 35 + 42 = 107$ tickets are given out.

Step 2: Take away the tickets from them. Students who have 2 or more tickets will give back 2 tickets. Students who have less than 2 tickets will give back all the tickets.

Step 3: Calculate the number of tickets taken back: at most $2 \times 52 = 104$ tickets were taken back.

Step 4: Calculate the number of tickets that are still in the students hands. $107 - 104 = 3$.

At this moment, any student who has the ticket will have only one ticket. These students are the ones who like 3 activities. The answer is 3.

Example 25. There are 100 students in a class. 75 of them like to play basketball. 80 like to play chess. 92 like to sing. 85 like to swim. At least how many students like all the 4 activities?

Solution: 32.

Method 1:

Number of students who like to play basketball and chess: $75 + 80 = 155$.

There are at least $155 - 100 = 55$ students who like to play both basketball and chess.

Similarly, there are at least $92 + 85 - 100 = 77$ students who like to sing and swim.

There are at least $55 + 77 - 100 = 32$ students who like all 4 activities.

Method 2: **The tickets method**

Step 1: Give each student a ticket for each activity he or she likes. There are $75 + 80 + 92 + 85 = 332$ tickets given out.

Step 2: Take away the tickets from them. Students who have 3 or more tickets will give back 3 tickets. Students who have less than 3 tickets will give back all the tickets.

Step 3: Calculate the number of tickets taken back: at most $3 \times 100 = 300$ tickets were taken back.

Step 4: Calculate the number of tickets that are still in the students hands.

$332 - 300 = 32$.

At this moment, any student who has the ticket will have only one ticket. These students are the ones who like 4 activities.

The answer is 32.

Example 26. Of the 60 students at Hope Middle School, 40 take algebra, 45 take geometry, 48 take trigonometry. Furthermore, 22 take all three courses. At most how many students take none of these courses?

Solution: 4.

Method 1:

The universal set $U = 60$. Let x be the number of students who take none of the courses. $60 - x$ is the number of students who take one or more courses.

Method 1: We use the ticket method to solve the problem.

Distribute $40 + 45 + 48 = 133$ tickets to these $60 - x$ students. Then we take back two tickets from each of those students. At most we can get $2 \times (60 - x)$ tickets back. We have $133 - 2 \times (60 - x) = 13 + 2x$ left which is equal to the number of students taking 3 courses.

Therefore, $13 + 2x = 22 \quad\Rightarrow\quad 2x = 9 \quad\Rightarrow\quad x = 4.5$

Since x is an integer, $x = 4$.

Method 2:

Figure (1) shows the Venn diagram of three events.

Figure (2) shows the case that we want to achieve (to get the greatest possible value for x).

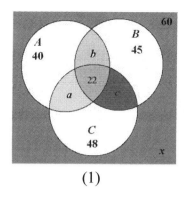 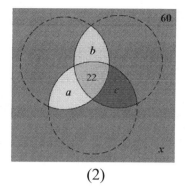

(1)   (2)

$$a + b + 22 = 40$$
$$b + c + 22 = 45$$
$$a + c + 22 = 48$$

$$a + b = 18$$
$$b + c = 23 \qquad\qquad \Rightarrow \qquad 2(a + b + c) = 67$$
$$a + c = 26$$

Since $(a + b + c)$ must be an integer, we modify the Venn diagram (2) as follows:

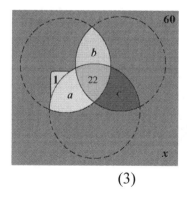

(3)

$$a + b + 22 + 1 = 40$$
$$b + c + 22 = 45$$
$$a + c + 22 = 48$$

$$a + b = 17$$
$$b + c = 23$$
$$a + c = 26$$
$$\Rightarrow \qquad 2(a + b + c) = 66 \qquad \Rightarrow \qquad a + b + c = 33$$

So $a = 10$, $b = 7$ and $c = 16$.

$x = 60 - 10 - 7 - 16 - 1 - 22 = 4$.

Figure (4) is one of the possible cases that work.

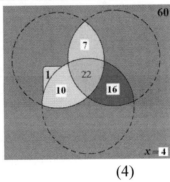

(4)

Problems involving finding n^{th} term

Example 27. (1988 National Target last problem) K is the set of natural numbers with the property that every element in K is not divisible by 4 and is not divisible by 7. Find the 79th smallest member of K.

Solution: 122.

The number of terms in K from 1 to 4×7 is

$$28 - \left\lfloor \frac{28}{4} \right\rfloor - \left\lfloor \frac{28}{7} \right\rfloor + \left\lfloor \frac{28}{4 \times 7} \right\rfloor = 28 - 7 - 4 + 1 = 18$$

So $a_1 = 1$, $a_2 = 2$, $a_3 = 3$, $a_4 = 5$, $a_5 = 6$, $a_6 = 9$, $a_7 = 10$, $a_8 = 11$, ..., $a_{18} = 27$.

We also have $a_{19} = 28 + 1$, $a_{20} = 28 + 2$, $a_{21} = 28 + 3$, ..., $a_{56} = 28 + 27$,... Since $79 = 18 \times 4 + 7$, So $a_{79} = 28 \times 4 + a_7 = 28 \times 4 + 10 = 122$.

122 is the answer.

Example 28. K is the set of natural numbers with the property that every element in K is not divisible by 3 and is not divisible by 4. But if a number is divisible by 3 or 4 and is also divisible by 5, the number is in K (like 15, 20, 60,…).. Find the 79th smallest member of K.

Solution: 133.

Method 1:

Let $a_{79} = n$.

$$79 = n - n(A \cap B) + n(A \cap C) + n(B \cap C) - n(A \cap B \cap C)$$

$$= n - \left\lfloor \frac{n}{3} \right\rfloor - \left\lfloor \frac{n}{4} \right\rfloor + \left\lfloor \frac{n}{3 \times 4} \right\rfloor + \left\lfloor \frac{n}{3 \times 5} \right\rfloor + \left\lfloor \frac{n}{4 \times 5} \right\rfloor - \left\lfloor \frac{n}{3 \times 4 \times 5} \right\rfloor \qquad (1)$$

We know that $x - 1 < \lfloor x \rfloor \leq x$.

So $79 < n - (\frac{n}{3} - 1) - (\frac{n}{4} - 1) + \frac{n}{3 \times 4} + \frac{n}{3 \times 5} + \frac{n}{4 \times 5} - (\frac{n}{3 \times 4 \times 5} - 1) = \frac{3}{5}n + 3 \qquad (2)$

and $79 > n - \frac{n}{3} - \frac{n}{4} + (\frac{n}{3 \times 4} - 1) + (\frac{n}{3 \times 5} - 1) + (\frac{n}{4 \times 5} - 1) - \frac{n}{3 \times 4 \times 5} = \frac{3}{5}n - 3 \qquad (3)$

From (2) and (3) we get $126\frac{2}{3} < n < 136\frac{2}{3}$ or $127 \leq n \leq 136$.

We know that n is neither a multiple of 3 nor 4 (except a multiple of 5), so n must be one of 127, 130, 131, 133, 134, 135.

Substituting these possible values into (1), we see that the only solution is $n = 133$.

Method 2:

The least common multiple of 3, 4, and 5 is 60.

$$60 - \left\lfloor \frac{60}{3} \right\rfloor - \left\lfloor \frac{60}{4} \right\rfloor + \left\lfloor \frac{60}{3 \times 4} \right\rfloor + \left\lfloor \frac{60}{3 \times 5} \right\rfloor + \left\lfloor \frac{60}{4 \times 5} \right\rfloor - \left\lfloor \frac{60}{3 \times 4 \times 5} \right\rfloor = 36 .$$

There are 36 terms in a_n from 1 to 60.

$a_1 = 1$, $a_2 = 2$, $a_3 = 5$, $a_4 = 7$, $a_5 = 10$, $a_6 = 11$ $a_7 = 13$, …, $a_{36} = 60$.

We know that $79 = 36 \times 2 + 7$. So $a_{79} = 60 \times 2 + a_7 = 120 + 13 = 133$.

Example 29. *K* is the set of natural numbers relatively prime to 105. Find the 142nd smallest member of *K*.

Solution: 311.

Method 1:

$105 = 3 \times 5 \times 7$.

Let $a_{79} = n$.

$$142 = n - \left\lfloor \frac{n}{3} \right\rfloor - \left\lfloor \frac{n}{5} \right\rfloor - \left\lfloor \frac{n}{7} \right\rfloor + \left\lfloor \frac{n}{3\times 5} \right\rfloor + \left\lfloor \frac{n}{3\times 7} \right\rfloor + \left\lfloor \frac{n}{5\times 7} \right\rfloor - \left\lfloor \frac{n}{3\times 5\times 7} \right\rfloor \qquad (1)$$

We know that $x - 1 < \lfloor x \rfloor \leq x$.

So $142 < n - (\frac{n}{3} - 1) - (\frac{n}{5} - 1) - (\frac{n}{7} - 1) + \frac{n}{3\times 5} + \frac{n}{3\times 7} + \frac{n}{5\times 7} - (\frac{n}{3\times 5\times 7} - 1) = \frac{16}{35}n + 4$

$\qquad (2)$

and $142 > n - \frac{n}{3} - \frac{n}{5} - \frac{n}{7} + (\frac{n}{3\times 5} - 1) + (\frac{n}{3\times 7} - 1) + (\frac{n}{5\times 7} - 1) - \frac{n}{3\times 4\times 5} = \frac{16}{35}n - 3$

$\qquad (3)$

From (2) and (3) we get $301\frac{7}{8} < n < 317\frac{3}{16}$ or $302 \leq n \leq 317$.

We know that *n* is relatively prime to 105, so *n* must be one of 302, 307, 308, 311, 313, 314, 316, 317.

Substituting $n = 317$ into (1), we see that

$$n - \left\lfloor \frac{n}{3} \right\rfloor - \left\lfloor \frac{n}{5} \right\rfloor - \left\lfloor \frac{n}{7} \right\rfloor + \left\lfloor \frac{n}{3\times 5} \right\rfloor + \left\lfloor \frac{n}{3\times 7} \right\rfloor + \left\lfloor \frac{n}{5\times 7} \right\rfloor - \left\lfloor \frac{n}{3\times 5\times 7} \right\rfloor = 146,$$ which is 4 more

than 142. So $n = 311$ should work and indeed and we see that

$$n - \left\lfloor \frac{n}{3} \right\rfloor - \left\lfloor \frac{n}{5} \right\rfloor - \left\lfloor \frac{n}{7} \right\rfloor + \left\lfloor \frac{n}{3\times 5} \right\rfloor + \left\lfloor \frac{n}{3\times 7} \right\rfloor + \left\lfloor \frac{n}{5\times 7} \right\rfloor - \left\lfloor \frac{n}{3\times 5\times 7} \right\rfloor = 142.$$

Method 2:

$105 = 3 \times 5 \times 7$.

The number of terms relatively prime to 105 from 1 to 105 is

$$105 - \left\lfloor \frac{105}{3} \right\rfloor - \left\lfloor \frac{105}{5} \right\rfloor - \left\lfloor \frac{105}{7} \right\rfloor + \left\lfloor \frac{105}{3 \times 5} \right\rfloor + \left\lfloor \frac{105}{3 \times 7} \right\rfloor + \left\lfloor \frac{105}{5 \times 7} \right\rfloor - \left\lfloor \frac{105}{3 \times 5 \times 7} \right\rfloor$$

$= 105 - (35 + 21 + 15) + (7 + 3 + 5) - 1 = 48.$

So $a_1 = 1$, $a_2 = 2$, $a_3 = 4,\ldots, a_{45} = 97$, $a_{46} = 101$, $a_{47} = 103$, and $a_{48} = 104$.

We also have $a_{49} = 105 + 1$, $a_{50} = 105 + 2$, $a_{51} = 105 + 4, \ldots, a_{96} = 105 + 104,\ldots$

Since $142 = 48 \times 2 + 46$, So $a_{142} = 105 \times 2 + a_{46} = 210 + 101 = 311.$

PROBLEMS

Problem 1. What is the probability that an integer in the set $\{1, 2, 3, \ldots, 100\}$ is divisible by 2 and not divisible by 3? (2005 AMC 10).

Problem 2. Find the number of integers from 1 to 300 inclusive that are divisible by neither 7 nor 8.

Problem 3. How many positive integers not exceeding 2001 are multiples of 3 or 4 but not 12?

Problem 4. How many integers between 1 and 600 inclusive are divisible by either 3, or 5, or 7?

Problem 5. How many positive integers less than or equal to 2001 are multiples of 3 or 4 but not 5?

Problem 6. How many positive integers less than or equal to 2001 are multiples of 3 or 4 but not 15?

Problem 7. How many positive integers less than or equal to 1992 are multiples of 3, but neither multiples of 2 nor 5?

Problem 8. (2008 Mathcounts State Sprint #25) How many integers between 1 and 200 are multiples of both 3 and 5 but not of either 4 or 7?

Problem 9. In a group of 30 people, 8 speak English, 12 speak Spanish and 10 speak French. It is known that 5 speak English and Spanish, 5 Spanish and French, and 7 English and French. The number of people speaking all three languages is 3. How many do not speak any of these languages?

Problem 10. (1997 Mathcounts National Target #3) Of 6000 apples harvested, every third apples was too small, every fourth was too green, and every tenth apple was bruised. The remaining apples were perfect. How many perfect apples were harvested?

Problem 11. Three rugs have a combined area of 200 m^2. By overlapping the rugs to cover a floor area of 140 m^2, the area which is covered by exactly two layers of rug is 24 m^2. What area of floor is covered by three layers of rug?

Problem 12. Alex, Bob and Charlie are watering 100 flowerpots. Alex watered 76 pots, Bob watered 69 pots, and Charlie watered 85 pots. At least how many flowerpots have been watered three times?

Problem 13. In a school of 100 students, 90 study English, 75 study Spanish and 42 study French. Every student study at least one of the three languages. What is the least possible number of students who could be studying all three languages?

Problem 14. From a group of 40 students, 28 are taking geometry, and 24 are taking science. Find the fewest number of students who could be taking both.

Problem 15. In a science class of 16 students, 11 students are on the basketball team, and 7 students are on the track team. What is the least number of students in this class who are on both teams? (Mathcounts Handbooks)

Problem 16. 8th grade classes are surveyed. 78% of the students like swimming, 80% like computer games, 84% like playing chess, and 88% like reading books. At most how many percent of students like all four activities?

Problem 17. Alex, Bob and Charlie are each reading a copy of the same book that contains 100 stories. Each person is reading in the order of the page numbers. Alex has read 75 stories. Bob has read 60 stories. Charlie has read 52 stories. At least how many stories have been read by all three kids?

Problem 18. Alex, Bob and Charlie are watering 50 flowerpots. Alex watered 35 pots, Bob watered 35 pots, and Charlie watered 35 pots. At least how many flowerpots have been watered three times?

Problem 19. Of the 100 students at Hope Middle School, 80 take algebra, 70 take geometry, 60 take trigonometry. Furthermore, 22 take all three courses. At most how many students take none of these courses?

Problem 20. There were 100 students taking in a math contest consisting of 4 questions. 90 of them got problem 1 correct. 85 of them got problem 2 correct. 60 of them got problem 3 correct. 40 of them got problem 4 correct. Anyone who got 3 or more problems correct advanced to the next round. At least how many students advanced to the next round?

Problem 21. There were 100 students taking in a math contest consisting of 4 questions. 90 of them got problem 1 correct. 85 of them got problem 2 correct. 60 of them got problem 3 correct. 15 of them got problem 4 correct. Anyone who got 3 or more problems correct advanced to the next round. At most how many students advanced to the next round?

Problem 22 (2014 Mathcounts National Target Problem4) . At a New York airport 135 international travelers were polled to see what language or languages each spoke. Of those polled, 87 spoke English; 86 spoke Spanish; 39 spoke French; 31 spoke English and Spanish, but not French; and 19 spoke English and French, but not Spanish. Only one person polled spoke Spanish and French but not English. If everyone spoke at least one of these three languages, how many travelers spoke all three languages?

Problem 23. Each of the 2015 students at a high school studies either Spanish or French, and some study both. The number who study Spanish is between 80 percent and 85 percent of the school population, and the number who study French is between 30 percent and 40 percent. Let m be the smallest number of students who could study both languages, and let M be the largest number of students who could study both languages. Find $M - m$.

Problem 24. Let S be the set of all rational numbers r, $0 < r < 1$, that have a repeating decimal expansion of the form $0.abababab\cdots = 0.\overline{ab}$, where the digits a, b are not necessarily distinct. To write the elements of S as fractions in lowest terms, how many different numerators are required?

Problem 25. K is the set of natural numbers with the property that every element in K is not divisible by 3 and is not divisible by 4. But if a number is divisible by 3 or 4 and is also divisible by 5, the number is in K (like 15, 20, 60,...).. Find the 2009th smallest member of K.

Problem 26. K is the set of natural numbers relatively prime to 105. Find the 1000th smallest member of K.

SOLUTIONS

Problem 1. Solution: 17/50.
The denominator of our fraction will obviously be 100, the total number of integers in our set. To determine the numerator, we must find how many integers from 1 to 100 are divisible by 2 and not divisible by 3.
Let A be the integers from 1 to 100 divisible by 2 and B be the set of integers from 1 to 100 divisible by 3.

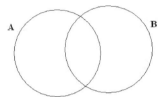

Our job is to find the shaded area of the figure below:

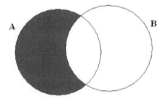

To find the shaded area, first we calculate the union of AB

$$n(A \cup B) = n(A) + n(B) - n(A \cap B) = \left\lfloor \frac{100}{2} \right\rfloor + \left\lfloor \frac{100}{3} \right\rfloor - \left\lfloor \frac{100}{2 \times 3} \right\rfloor = 50 + 33 - 16 = 67$$

Next, we subtract the set B:

$$67 - \left\lfloor \frac{100}{3} \right\rfloor = 67 - 33 = 34$$

So there are 34 integers that are divisible by 2 and not divisible by 3.

The final solution is then $\dfrac{34}{100} = \dfrac{17}{50}$.

Problem 2. Solution: 226.
Let A be the integers from 1 to 300 divisible by 7 and B be the set of integers from 1 to 300 divisible by 8. The number of positive integers less than or equal to 300

that are divisible by either 7 or 8 is the union of set A and set B can be calculated by

$$n(A \cup B) = n(A) + n(B) - n(A \cap B) = \left\lfloor \frac{300}{7} \right\rfloor + \left\lfloor \frac{300}{8} \right\rfloor - \left\lfloor \frac{300}{7 \times 8} \right\rfloor = 42 + 37 - 5 = 74$$

$$300 - n(A \cup B) = 300 - 74 = 226.$$

Problem 3. Solution: 835.

Method 1: Let circle A represents the set of numbers divisible by 3, and circle B represents the set of numbers divisible by 4.

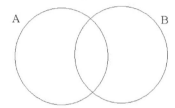

For this question, our job is to find the shaded area.

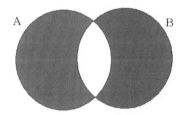

To find the shaded region, first we find the union of sets A and B, and then remove the intersection of A and B.

$$\left\lfloor \frac{2001}{3} \right\rfloor + \left\lfloor \frac{2001}{4} \right\rfloor - \left\lfloor \frac{2001}{3 \times 4} \right\rfloor - \left\lfloor \frac{2001}{3 \times 4} \right\rfloor = 667 + 500 - 166 - 166 = 835.$$

Method 2:

$$\left\lfloor\frac{2001}{3}\right\rfloor+\left\lfloor\frac{2001}{4}\right\rfloor+\left\lfloor\frac{2001}{12}\right\rfloor-\left\lfloor\frac{2001}{3\times4}\right\rfloor-\left\lfloor\frac{2001}{LCM(3,12)}\right\rfloor-\left\lfloor\frac{2001}{LCM(4,12)}\right\rfloor+$$

$$\left\lfloor\frac{2001}{LCM(3,4,12)}\right\rfloor-\left\lfloor\frac{2001}{12}\right\rfloor$$

$$=\left\lfloor\frac{2001}{3}\right\rfloor+\left\lfloor\frac{2001}{4}\right\rfloor-\left\lfloor\frac{2001}{3\times4}\right\rfloor-\left\lfloor\frac{2001}{LCM(3,12)}\right\rfloor-\left\lfloor\frac{2001}{LCM(4,12)}\right\rfloor+\left\lfloor\frac{2001}{LCM(3,4,12)}\right\rfloor$$

$$=\left\lfloor\frac{2001}{3}\right\rfloor+\left\lfloor\frac{2001}{4}\right\rfloor-\left\lfloor\frac{2001}{3\times4}\right\rfloor-\left\lfloor\frac{2001}{12}\right\rfloor-\left\lfloor\frac{2001}{12}\right\rfloor+\left\lfloor\frac{2001}{12}\right\rfloor$$

$$=\left\lfloor\frac{2001}{3}\right\rfloor+\left\lfloor\frac{2001}{4}\right\rfloor-\left\lfloor\frac{2001}{3\times4}\right\rfloor-\left\lfloor\frac{2001}{3\times4}\right\rfloor=835.$$

Problem 4. Solution: 325.

$$\left\lfloor\frac{600}{3}\right\rfloor+\left\lfloor\frac{600}{5}\right\rfloor+\left\lfloor\frac{600}{7}\right\rfloor-\left\lfloor\frac{600}{3\times5}\right\rfloor-\left\lfloor\frac{600}{3\times7}\right\rfloor-\left\lfloor\frac{600}{5\times7}\right\rfloor+\left\lfloor\frac{600}{3\times5\times7}\right\rfloor$$

$$=200 + 120 + 85 - 40 - 28 - 17 + 5 = 325 .$$

Problem 5. Solution: 801.

Let circle A represent the set of numbers divisible by 3, circle B represent the set of numbers divisible by 5, and circle C represent the set of numbers divisible by 4.

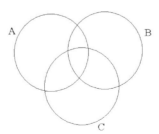

Our job is to find the shaded area in the figure below.

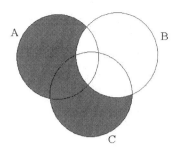

To find the shaded area, we find the union of sets A, B and C, and then subtract that from the set B to get the final result.

$$\left\lfloor\frac{2001}{3}\right\rfloor+\left\lfloor\frac{2001}{4}\right\rfloor+\left\lfloor\frac{2001}{5}\right\rfloor-\left\lfloor\frac{2001}{3\times4}\right\rfloor-\left\lfloor\frac{2001}{3\times5}\right\rfloor-\left\lfloor\frac{2001}{4\times5}\right\rfloor+\left\lfloor\frac{2001}{3\times4\times5}\right\rfloor-\left\lfloor\frac{2001}{5}\right\rfloor$$

$$=\left\lfloor\frac{2001}{3}\right\rfloor+\left\lfloor\frac{2001}{4}\right\rfloor-\left\lfloor\frac{2001}{3\times4}\right\rfloor-\left\lfloor\frac{2001}{3\times5}\right\rfloor-\left\lfloor\frac{2001}{4\times5}\right\rfloor+\left\lfloor\frac{2001}{3\times4\times5}\right\rfloor.$$

$$= 667 + 500 - 166 - 133 - 100 + 33 = 801.$$

Problem 6. Solution: 868.

Let circle A represent the set of numbers divisible by 3, circle B represent the set of numbers divisible by 15, and circle C represent the set of numbers divisible by 4.

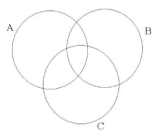

Our job is to find the shaded area in the figure below.

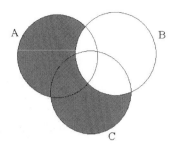

This question is similar to the previous one, but note that here we use a different way to tackle the problem.

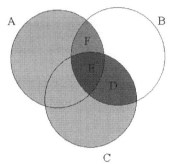

We calculate the area of $A \bigcup C - (E \bigcup D) - (E \bigcup F) + E$:

$$A \bigcup C = \left\lfloor \frac{2001}{3} \right\rfloor + \left\lfloor \frac{2001}{4} \right\rfloor - \left\lfloor \frac{2001}{3 \times 4} \right\rfloor,$$

$$E \bigcup D = \left\lfloor \frac{2001}{4 \times 15} \right\rfloor,$$

$$E \bigcup F = \left\lfloor \frac{2001}{LCM(3,15)} \right\rfloor,$$

$$E = \left\lfloor \frac{2001}{LCM(3,4,15)} \right\rfloor.$$

Using the Inclusion – Exclusion Theorem, our answer will be:

$$\left\lfloor \frac{2001}{3} \right\rfloor + \left\lfloor \frac{2001}{4} \right\rfloor - \left\lfloor \frac{2001}{3\times 4} \right\rfloor - \left\lfloor \frac{2001}{4\times 15} \right\rfloor - \left\lfloor \frac{2001}{LCM(3,15)} \right\rfloor + \left\lfloor \frac{2001}{LCM(3,4,15)} \right\rfloor$$

$$= 667 + 500 - 166 - 33 - 133 + 33 = 868.$$

Problem 7. Solution: 266.

Method 1: Let circle A represent the set of numbers divisible by 3, circle B represent the set of numbers divisible by 2, and circle C represent the set of numbers divisible by 5.

Our job is to find the shaded area of the figure below:

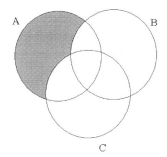

(1) Find A: $\left\lfloor \dfrac{1992}{3} \right\rfloor$

(2) Find $D \cup E$: $\left\lfloor \dfrac{1992}{3\times 5} \right\rfloor$

(3) Find $E \cup F$: $\left\lfloor \dfrac{1992}{3\times 2} \right\rfloor$

(4) Find E: $\left\lfloor \dfrac{1992}{3\times 2\times 5} \right\rfloor$

(5) $A - (D \cup E) - (E \cup F) + E$ is the final answer to the question.

$$\left\lfloor \frac{1992}{3} \right\rfloor - \left\lfloor \frac{2001}{3\times 2} \right\rfloor - \left\lfloor \frac{1992}{3\times 5} \right\rfloor + \left\lfloor \frac{1992}{3\times 2\times 5} \right\rfloor = 664 - 332 - 132 + 66 = 266.$$

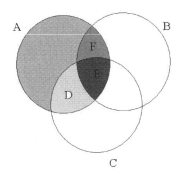

Method 2:

(1) Calculate the union, $n(A \cup B \cup C) = 1462$.

(2) Calculate (B or C), $n(B \cup C) = 1195$.

(3) $n(A \cup B \cup C) - n(B \cup C) = 266$ is the number of positive integers less than or equal to 1992 that are multiples of 3, but neither multiples of 2 nor 5.

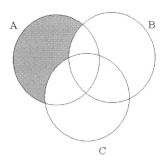

Problem 8. Solution: 9.

Let circle A represent the set of numbers divisible by 15 (3 × 5), circle B represent the set of numbers divisible by 4, and circle C represent the set of numbers divisible by 7.

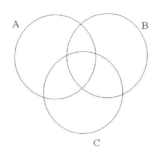

Our job is to find the shaded area of the figure below:

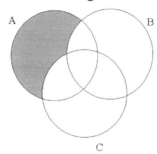

We follow the steps below:

Step 1: Calculate the union using PIE:

$n(A \cup B \cup C) = n(A) + n(B) + n(C) - n(A \cap B) - n(B \cap C) - n(C \cap A) + n(A \cap B \cap C)$
$= 13 + 50 + 28 - 3 - 1 - 7 = 80$

Step 2: Calculate (B or C).

$n(B \cup C) = n(B) + n(C) - n(B \cap C)$
$= 50 + 28 - 7 = 71$

Step 3: (1) – (2) will be the desired answer, which is 80 – 71 = 9.

Problem 9. Solution: 14.

$n(A \cup B \cup C) = n(A) + n(B) + n(C) - n(A \cap B) - n(B \cap C) - n(C \cap A) + n(A \cap B \cap C)$
$= 8 + 12 + 10 - 5 - 5 - 7 + 3 = 16.$

Because we want to find the number of people who don't speak any of the three languages, we subtract 16 from the total, 30, to obtain our answer 14.

Problem 10. Solution: 2800.
Let N be the number of apples that are not perfect. Then

$$N = \left\lfloor \frac{6000}{3} \right\rfloor + \left\lfloor \frac{6000}{4} \right\rfloor + \left\lfloor \frac{6000}{10} \right\rfloor - \left(\left\lfloor \frac{6000}{3 \times 4} \right\rfloor + \left\lfloor \frac{6000}{3 \times 10} \right\rfloor + \left\lfloor \frac{6000}{LCM(4,10)} \right\rfloor \right) + \left\lfloor \frac{6000}{LCM(3,4,10)} \right\rfloor$$

$$= 3200.$$

We want to find the number of apples that are perfect, so the solution will be:
Total apples $- N = 6000 - 3200 = 2800$.

Problem 11. Solution: 18.
$$n(A \cup B \cup C) = n(A) + n(B) + n(C) - n(A \cap B) - n(B \cap C) - n(C \cap A) + n(A \cap B \cap C)$$
We know that $n(A \cup B \cup C) = 140$,

$$n(A) + n(B) + n(C) = 200.$$

Let $n(A \cap B \cap C) = k$.
$$n(A \cap B) + n(B \cap C) + n(C \cap A) = a + k + b + k + c + k$$

We have: $140 = 200 - (a + b + c + 3k) + k$

or $140 = 200 - (24 + 3k) + k$

$k = 18$. Thus, the area of floor covered by exactly three layers of rug is 18m^2.

Problem 12. Solution: 30.
The tickets method
Step 1: Give each flowerpot a ticket for each watering. $76 + 69 + 85 = 230$ tickets
are given out.

Step 2: Take away the tickets from the flowerpots. The pots that received 2 or
more tickets will give back 2 tickets. The pots that received less than 2 tickets will
give back all the tickets.

Step 3: Calculate the number of tickets taken back: at most $2 \times 100 = 200$ tickets were taken back.

Step 4: Calculate the number of tickets that are still with the flowerpots.
$230 - 200 = 30$.
At this moment, any flowerpot that has the ticket will have only one ticket. These pots are the ones that have been watering 3 times. The answer is 30.

Problem 13. Solution: 7.
The tickets method
$90 + 75 + 42 = 207$.
$207 - 100 - 100 = 7$.

Problem 14. Solution:12.
The tickets method
$28 + 24 = 52$.
$52 - 40 = 12$.

Problem 15. Solution: 2.
The tickets method
$11 + 7 = 18$.
$18 - 16 = 2$.

Problem 16. Solution: 78.
We draw 5 circles representing the percentages of the students like each activity in such a way that we can get most percent of students like all four activities. The answer is 78.

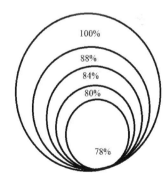

Problem 17. Solution: 12.

There are $75 + 60 - 100 = 35$ stories read by both Alex and Bob.

There are $75 + 52 - 100 = 27$ stories read by both Alex and Charlie.

There are $60 + 52 - 100 = 12$ stories read by both Bob and Charlie. So at least 12 stories have been read by all three kids.

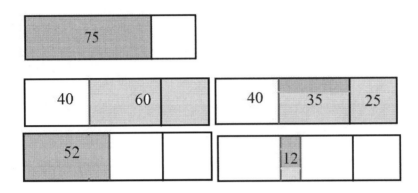

Problem 18. Solution: 5.

The tickets method

$35 + 35 + 35 - 50 \times 2 = 5$.

Problem 19. Solution: 6.

The universal set $U = 100$. Let x be the number of students who take none of the courses. $100 - x$ is the number of students who take one or more courses.

We use the ticket method to solve the problem.

Distribute $80 + 70 + 60 = 210$ tickets to these $100 - x$ students. Then we take back two tickets from each of those students. At most we can get $2 \times (100 - x)$ tickets back. We have $210 - 2 \times (100 - x) = 10 + 2x$ left which is equal to the number of students taking 3 courses.

Therefore, $10 + 2x = 22 \quad \Rightarrow \quad 2x = 12 \quad \Rightarrow \quad x = 6$

Problem 20. Solution: 38.

We use the ticket method.

$90 + 85 + 60 + 40 = 275$

$275 - 100 - 100 = 75$.

Since we like to find the smallest number of students advanced to the next round, we assume that the students left each has two tickets (they each answered 4 questions correct).

$75 / 2 = 37.5$. So the answer is 38 (37 answered 4 questions correct and 1 answered 3 questions correct).

Problem 21. Solution: 50.

We use the ticket method.

$90 + 85 + 60 + 15 = 250$

$250 - 100 - 100 = 50$.

Since we like to find the greatest number of students advanced to the next round, we assume that the students left each has one ticket.

So the answer is 50.

Problem 22 Solution: 13.

Method 1:

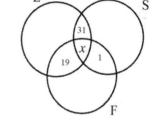

$n(A \cup B \cup C) = n(A) + n(B) + n(C)$

$- n(A \cap B) - n(B \cap C) - n(C \cap A) + n(A \cap B \cap C)$

$135 = 87 + 86 + 39 - (31 + x) - (19 + x) - (1 + x) + x \Rightarrow$

$\qquad 135 = 161 - 2x \Rightarrow \qquad 2x = 26 \Rightarrow \qquad x = 13.$

Method 2:

$A + 31 + x + 19 = 87$ $\qquad\qquad$ (1)

$B + 31 + x + 1 = 86$ $\qquad\qquad$ (2)

$C + 1 + x + 19 = 39$ $\qquad\qquad$ (3)

$A + 31 + x + B + 19 + 1 + C = 135$ $\qquad$ (4)

$(1) + (2) + (3): A + B + C + 3x + 102 = 212$ $\qquad$ (5)

$(5) - (4): 2x + 51 = 77 \qquad \Rightarrow \qquad 2x + 51 = 26$

$\Rightarrow \qquad x = 13.$

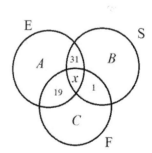

Problem 23. Solution: 302.

$M = \lfloor 0.85 \times 2015 \rfloor + \lfloor 0.40 \times 2015 \rfloor - 2015 = 1712 + 806 - 2015 = 503.$

$$m = \lfloor 0.80 \times 2015 \rfloor + \lfloor 0.30 \times 2015 \rfloor - 2015 = 1612 + 604 - 2015 = 201$$
$$M - m = 503 - 201 = 302 \,.$$

Problem 24. Solution: 63.

$$0.\overline{ab} = \frac{ab}{99}$$

$$99 = 3^2 \times 11.$$

We have two cases:

Case 1: The two-digit number ab is neither divisible by 3 nor 11. In this case, the

fraction $\dfrac{ab}{3^2 \times 11}$ is in lowest terms.

The number of such different numerators is

$$99 - \left(\left\lfloor \frac{99}{3} \right\rfloor + \left\lfloor \frac{99}{11} \right\rfloor - \left\lfloor \frac{99}{3 \times 11} \right\rfloor \right) = 99 - (33 + 9 - 3) = 60 \,.$$

Case 2: The two-digit number ab is a multiple of 3 or 11: $\dfrac{k}{11}, \dfrac{l}{3^2}$, or $\dfrac{l}{3}$, where k

is a multiple of 3 and l is a multiple of 11.

Since we want the fractions, there is no possible value for l.

The fraction $\dfrac{ab}{3^2 \times 11}$ can be reduced as $\dfrac{3}{11}, \dfrac{6}{11}$, and $\dfrac{9}{11}$ (when $k = 3, 6, 9$)

The answer is $60 + 3 = 63$.

Problem 25. Solution: 3347.

Method 1:

Let $a_{2009} = n$.

$$2009 = n - n(A \cup B) + n(A \cap C) + n(B \cap C) - n(A \cap B \cap C)$$

$$= n - \left\lfloor \frac{n}{3} \right\rfloor - \left\lfloor \frac{n}{4} \right\rfloor + \left\lfloor \frac{n}{3 \times 4} \right\rfloor + \left\lfloor \frac{n}{3 \times 5} \right\rfloor + \left\lfloor \frac{n}{4 \times 5} \right\rfloor - \left\lfloor \frac{n}{3 \times 4 \times 5} \right\rfloor \qquad (1)$$

We know that $x - 1 < \lfloor x \rfloor \le x$.

So $2009 < n - (\frac{n}{3} - 1) - (\frac{n}{4} - 1) + \frac{n}{3 \times 4} + \frac{n}{3 \times 5} + \frac{n}{4 \times 5} - (\frac{n}{3 \times 4 \times 5} - 1) = \frac{3}{5} n + 3$ (2)

and $2009 > n - \frac{n}{3} - \frac{n}{4} + (\frac{n}{3 \times 4} - 1) + (\frac{n}{3 \times 5} - 1) + (\frac{n}{4 \times 5} - 1) - \frac{n}{3 \times 4 \times 5} = \frac{3}{5} n - 3$ (3)

From (2) and (3) we get $3343\frac{1}{3} < n < 3353\frac{1}{3}$ or $3344 \le n \le 3353$.

We know that n is neither a multiple of 3 nor 4 (except a multiple of 5), so n must be one of 3345, 3346, 3347, 3349, 3350, 3353.

Substituting these possible values into (1), we see that the only solution is $n = 3347$.

Method 2:

The least common multiple of 3, 4, and 5 is 60.

$$60 - \left\lfloor \frac{60}{3} \right\rfloor - \left\lfloor \frac{60}{4} \right\rfloor + \left\lfloor \frac{60}{3 \times 4} \right\rfloor + \left\lfloor \frac{60}{3 \times 5} \right\rfloor + \left\lfloor \frac{60}{4 \times 5} \right\rfloor - \left\lfloor \frac{60}{3 \times 4 \times 5} \right\rfloor = 36.$$

There are 36 terms in a_n from 1 to 60.

$a_1 = 1$, $a_2 = 2$, $a_3 = 5$, $a_4 = 7$, ..., $a_{29} = 47$,..., $a_{36} = 60$.

We know that $2009 = 36 \times 55 + 29$. So $a_{2009} = 60 \times 55 + a_{29} = 60 \times 55 + 47 = 3347$.

Problem 26. Solution: 2186.

$105 = 3 \times 5 \times 7$.

Let $a_{1000} = n$.

$$1000 = n - \left\lfloor \frac{n}{3} \right\rfloor - \left\lfloor \frac{n}{5} \right\rfloor - \left\lfloor \frac{n}{7} \right\rfloor + \left\lfloor \frac{n}{3 \times 5} \right\rfloor + \left\lfloor \frac{n}{3 \times 7} \right\rfloor + \left\lfloor \frac{n}{5 \times 7} \right\rfloor - \left\lfloor \frac{n}{3 \times 5 \times 7} \right\rfloor \qquad (1)$$

We know that $x - 1 < \lfloor x \rfloor \le x$.

So $1000 < n - (\frac{n}{3} - 1) - (\frac{n}{5} - 1) - (\frac{n}{7} - 1) + \frac{n}{3 \times 5} + \frac{n}{3 \times 7} + \frac{n}{5 \times 7} - (\frac{n}{3 \times 5 \times 7} - 1)$ (2)

and $1000 > n - \frac{n}{3} - \frac{n}{5} - \frac{n}{7} + (\frac{n}{3 \times 5} - 1) + (\frac{n}{3 \times 7} - 1) + (\frac{n}{5 \times 7} - 1) - \frac{n}{3 \times 4 \times 5}$ (3)

From (2) and (3) we get $2178\frac{3}{4} < n < 2194\frac{1}{16}$ or $3344 \le n \le 3353$.

We know that n is relatively prime t 105, so n must be one of 2176, 2182, 2183, 2186, 2188, 2189, 2192, 2194.

Substituting these possible values into (1), we see that the only solution is $n = 2186$.

Method 2:

$105 = 3 \times 5 \times 7$.

The number of terms relatively prime to 105 from 1 to 105 is

$$105 - \left\lfloor \frac{105}{3} \right\rfloor - \left\lfloor \frac{105}{5} \right\rfloor - \left\lfloor \frac{105}{7} \right\rfloor + \left\lfloor \frac{105}{3 \times 5} \right\rfloor + \left\lfloor \frac{105}{3 \times 7} \right\rfloor + \left\lfloor \frac{105}{5 \times 7} \right\rfloor - \left\lfloor \frac{105}{3 \times 5 \times 7} \right\rfloor$$

$= 105 - (35 + 21 + 15) + (7 + 3 + 5) - 1 = 48$.

So $a_1 = 1$, $a_2 = 2$, $a_3 = 4,\ldots$, $a_{40} = 86$, $a_{41} = 88$, $a_{42} = 89$, $a_{43} = 92$, $a_{44} = 94$, $a_{45} = 97$, $a_{46} = 101$, $a_{47} = 103$, and $a_{48} = 104$.

We also have $a_{49} = 105 + 1$, $a_{50} = 105 + 2$, $a_{51} = 105 + 4$, $\ldots$, $a_{96} = 105 + 104,\ldots$

Since $1000 = 48 \times 20 + 40$, So $a_{1000} = 105 \times 55 + a_{40} = 105 \times 55 + 86 = 2186$.

1. PYTHAGOREAN THEOREM

(For right triangles only): $a^2 + b^2 = c^2$ (1.1)

(*a* and *b* are two legs. *c* is the hypotenuse).

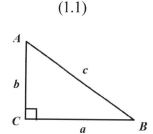

Proof:

Method 1: (Chinese way):

Arrange four congruent right triangles to form a square as show in the figure.

The area of the four triangles is $\dfrac{1}{2} a \times b \times 4 = 2ab$ (1)

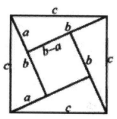

The area of the smaller square is $(b-a)^2 = b^2 - 2ab + a^2$ (2)

The area of the large square is c^2 (3)

(3) = (1) + (2)

$$c^2 = \dfrac{1}{2} a \times b \times 4 + (b-a)^2 = 2ab + b^2 - 2ab + a^2 \quad \Rightarrow \quad c^2 = a^2 + b^2$$

Method 2: (U.S. President Garfield's way):

Arrange two congruent right triangles as show in the figure. Connect PQ. Quadrilateral $ABQP$ is a trapezoid.

Since $\angle PRA + \angle QRB = 90°$, so $\angle PRQ = 90°$ and $\triangle PRQ$ is a right triangle.

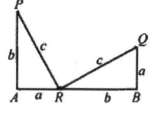

The two bases of the trapezoid are a and b.

The height is $(a + b)$. The area of trapezoid $ABQP$ is

$$S_{ABQP} = \dfrac{(a+b) \times (a+b)}{2}$$ (1)

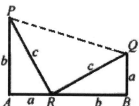

The sum of the areas of three right triangles

$$S = \dfrac{1}{2} ab + \dfrac{1}{2} ab + \dfrac{1}{2} c^2$$ (2)

We know that (1) = (2).

$$\frac{(a+b)\times(a+b)}{2} = \frac{1}{2}ab + \frac{1}{2}ab + \frac{1}{2}c^2 \;\Rightarrow\; a^2 + 2ab + b^2 = ab + ab + c^2 \Rightarrow$$

$$c^2 = a^2 + b^2$$

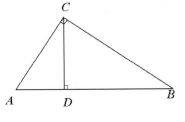

Method 3 (the simplest way).

In right triangle ABC, draw $CD \perp AB$. We know that

$\Delta ABC \sim \Delta ACD \sim \Delta CBD$ and:

$$AC^2 = AB \times AD \qquad\qquad (1)$$

$$BC^2 = AB \times BD \qquad\qquad (2)$$

$(1) + (2)$: $AC^2 + BC^2 = AB \times AD + AB \times BD = AB(AD + BD) = AB \times AB = AB^2$

Method 4:

In right triangle ABC, draw $CD \perp AB$. From the lecture 26, we know that $\Delta ABC \sim$

$\Delta ACD \sim \Delta CBD$.

We also know that $S_{\Delta CBD} + S_{\Delta ACD} = S_{\Delta ABC} \qquad \Rightarrow$

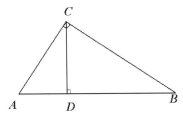

$$\frac{S_{\Delta CBD}}{S_{\Delta ABC}} + \frac{S_{\Delta ACD}}{S_{\Delta ABC}} = 1$$

$$(\frac{BC}{AB})^2 + (\frac{AC}{AB})^2 = 1 \;\Rightarrow\; (\frac{a}{c})^2 + (\frac{b}{c})^2 = 1$$

$$\Rightarrow \qquad a^2 + b^2 = c^2$$

2. SOME THEOREMS

Theorem 1.

When we draw similar figures on the two legs and the hypotenuse of a right triangle, the following formula is true:

$$S_1 = S_2 + S_3 \qquad\qquad (2.1)$$

Proof:

$$\frac{S_2}{S_1} = \left(\frac{a}{c}\right)^2 \qquad (1)$$

$$\frac{S_3}{S_1} = \left(\frac{b}{c}\right)^2 \qquad (2)$$

$$S_2 + S_3 = \frac{a^2 + b^2}{c^2} S_1 = S_1.$$

Theorem 2.
Draw semicircles along the sides of a right triangle, using the sides of the right triangle as the diameters, the following relationship is true:

$$S_1 = S_2 + S_3 \qquad\qquad (2.2)$$

Proof:
Since triangle ABC is a right triangle, we have:
$$a^2 + b^2 = c^2 \qquad (1)$$

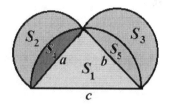

Multiplying every term of (1) by $\frac{1}{2}\pi\left(\frac{1}{2}\right)^2$:

$$\frac{1}{2}\pi\left(\frac{a}{2}\right)^2 + \frac{1}{2}\pi\left(\frac{b}{2}\right)^2 = \frac{1}{2}\pi\left(\frac{c}{2}\right)^2 \qquad (2)$$

Subtract $(S_4 + S_5)$ in each side of (2):

$$\frac{1}{2}\pi\left(\frac{a}{2}\right)^2 - S_4 + \frac{1}{2}\pi\left(\frac{b}{2}\right)^2 - S_5 = \frac{1}{2}\pi\left(\frac{c}{2}\right)^2 - S_4 - S_5 \qquad\Rightarrow\qquad S_2 + S_3 = S_1.$$

Theorem 3.
In a $45^\circ - 45^\circ - 90^\circ$ right triangle, or *right isosceles* triangle, the length of the hypotenuse is $\sqrt{2}$ times of the length of each leg.

104

Theorem 4. If triangle ABC is a right triangle, then the radius of the inscribed circle can be calculated by:

$$r = \frac{AC + BC - AB}{2}$$ (2.3)

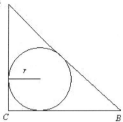

Theorem 5. For a right triangle, if $\angle A = 30°$, then

$$BC = \frac{1}{2} AB$$ (2.4)

$$AC = \frac{\sqrt{3}}{2} AB$$ (2.5)

$$AB = \frac{2\sqrt{3}}{3} AC$$ (2.6)

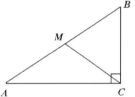

Theorem 6. The length of the median to the hypotenuse of a right triangle equals one-half the length of the hypotenuse.
$AM = MB = MC$

3. PYTHAGOREAN TRIPLES

A Pythagorean triple is an ordered triple (a, b, c) of three positive integers such that $a^2 + b^2 = c^2$. If a, b, and c are relatively prime, then the triple is called primitive.

Integral values of a, b, and c, where a, b, and c are relatively prime:

a	b	c		a	b	c
3	4	5		5	12	13
8	15	17		7	24	25
20	21	29		12	35	37
9	40	41		11	60	61
13	84	85		15	112	113

4. PROBLEM SOLVING SKILLS

4.1. Triangle and circle

Example 1. The two tangent circles with the radii 3 and 1, respectively, have an external common tangent as shown. Find the shaded area. Express your answer in terms of π.

Solution: $4\sqrt{3} - \dfrac{11}{6}\pi$.

We see that $DF = DA - AF = DA - BC = 3 - 1 = 2$.
$DC = 3 + 1 = 4$.
Thus triangle DCF is a $30° - 60° - 90°$ right triangle.
The shaded area is the area of the trapezoid $ABCD$ – the areas of sectors ADE and ECB.
The answer is

$$\frac{(3+1)\times\sqrt{4^2-2^2}}{2} - \frac{\pi\times3^2}{6} - \frac{\pi\times1^2}{3}$$

$$= 4\sqrt{3} - \frac{11}{6}\pi .$$

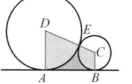 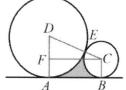

Example 2. Square $ABCD$ has side length 4. A semicircle with diameter AB is constructed inside the square, and the tangent to the semicircle from C intersects side AD at E. What is the length of AE?

Solution: 1.
Method 1:
 Let F be the point at which CE is tangent to the semicircle and let $AE = x$. Because CF and CB are both tangents to the semicircle, $CF = CB = 4$.

Similarly, $EA = EF = x$.
The Pythagorean Theorem applied to $\triangle CDE$ gives

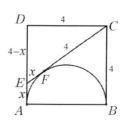

$(4-x)^2 + 4^2 = (4+x)^2$.
It follows that $x = 1$.

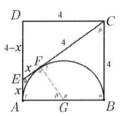

Method 2:
Connect GF. G is the center of the circle.
Quadrilaterals $BCFG$ and $FGAE$ are similar.

So we have $\dfrac{BC}{FG} = \dfrac{BG}{EF} \Rightarrow \dfrac{4}{2} = \dfrac{2}{x} \Rightarrow x = 1$.

Method 3:
The three sides of the triangle CDE are in the proportions of
3:4:5. Since $DC = 4$, DE must be 3 and CE must be 5. Thus x
must be 1.

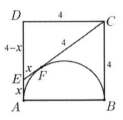

4.2. Triangle and quadrilateral

Example 3. (1999 Mathcounts State Sprint) Two vertical poles are 16 feet apart.
What is the minimum number of feet in the length of a rope that connects the top
of the 50-foot pole to the top of the 20-foot pole?

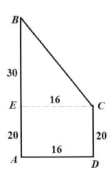

Solution: 34.
As shown in the figure below, triangle BCE is a right triangle
with legs of length 30 and 16. The minimum number of feet in
the length of a rope (BC), the hypotenuse, is calculated by
Pythagorean Theorem:

$BC^2 = EC^2 + BE^2 = 16^2 + 30^2 = 1156$

$\Rightarrow \quad BC = \sqrt{EC^2 + BE^2} = \sqrt{1156} = 34$.

Example 4. Quadrilateral $ABCD$ is a trapezoid, $AD = 17$, $AB = 30$, $BC = 25$, and
the altitude is 15. Find the area of the trapezoid.

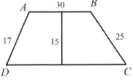

Solution: 660.

Let E and F be the feet of the perpendicular from A and B to DC, respectively.
Applying Pythagorean Theorem to right $\triangle AED$,
$DE^2 = AD^2 - AE^2 = 17^2 - 15^2 = 8^2$. So $DE = 8$.
Applying Pythagorean Theorem to right $\triangle BFC$,
$CF^2 = BC^2 - BF^2 = 25^2 - 15^2 = 20^2$.
So $CF = 20$. Thus $DC = 8 + 30 + 20 = 58$.

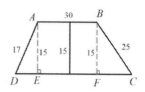

The trapezoid has area $\dfrac{30 + 58}{2} \times 15 = 660$.

Example 5. (2014 Mathcounts National Sprint Problem 30) The area of the largest equilateral triangle that can be inscribed in a square of side length 1 unit can be expressed in the form $a\sqrt{b} - c$ units^2, where a, b and c are integers. What is the value of $a + b + c$?

Solution: 8.

As shown in the figure, the largest equilateral triangle that can be inscribed in a square should be inscribed that way.

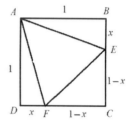

We have $1^2 + x^2 = (1-x)^2 + (1-x)^2 \implies x = 2 - \sqrt{3}$.

The area of equilateral triangle is
$$1^2 - \frac{1 \times x}{2} \times 2 - \frac{(1-x)^2}{2} = 1 - (2 - \sqrt{3}) - (2 - \sqrt{3}) = 2\sqrt{3} - 3$$
$a + b + c = 2 + 3 + 3 = 8$.

Example 6. (1989 National Target) A square $ABCD$ has line segments drawn from vertex B to the midpoints N and M of sides AD and DC respectively. Find the ratio of the perimeter of quadrilateral $BMDN$ to the perimeter of square $ABCD$. Express your answer in simplest radical form.

Solution: $\dfrac{\sqrt{5} + 1}{4}$.

ABCD is a square and *N* and *M* are midpoints of *AD* and *DC*, respectively.
Let *AN* = *x*. Then *ND* = *DM* = *MC* = *x* and *AB* = *BC*
= *CD* = *DA* = 2*x*.
Δ*BAN* is a right triangle with legs of lengths *BA* = 2*x*
and *AN* = *x*.
So $BN^2 = BA^2 + AN^2 = (2x)^2 + (x)^2 = 5x^2$
$BN = x\sqrt{5}$

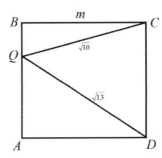

Similarly, $MB = x\sqrt{5}$.
So Perimeter of *BMDN* / Perimeter of *ABCD* = (*BN* + *ND* + *DM* + *MB*)/(

$$AB + BC + CD + DA) = \frac{x\sqrt{5}+x+x+x\sqrt{5}}{2x+2x+2x+2x} = \frac{2x\sqrt{5}+2x}{8x} = \frac{\sqrt{5}+1}{4}.$$

Example 7. (2015 Mathcounts Handbook) If point *Q* lies on side *AB* of square
ABCD such that $QC = \sqrt{10}$ units and $QD = \sqrt{13}$ units,
what is the area of square *ABCD*?

Solution: 9.

Let the side be *m*.

We know that $BC + BQ > \sqrt{10}$ and $QA + AD > \sqrt{13}$.

So $BC + BQ + QA + AD > \sqrt{10} + \sqrt{13}$ or
$3m > 3 + 3 = 6$. So *m* > 2 and $m^2 > 4$.

Applying Pythagorean Theorem to right triangle *BCQ*: $BQ^2 = QC^2 - BC^2 \Rightarrow$

$$BQ = \sqrt{QC^2 - BC^2} = \sqrt{10-m^2} \qquad (1)$$

Applying Pythagorean Theorem to right triangle *ADQ* :

$$AQ^2 = QD^2 - AD^2 \quad \Rightarrow \quad AQ = \sqrt{QD^2 - AD^2} = \sqrt{13-m^2} \quad (2)$$

(1) + (2): $BQ + AQ == m = \sqrt{10-m^2} + \sqrt{13-m^2} \qquad (3)$

Re-write (3) as $\sqrt{13-m^2} = m - \sqrt{10-m^2} \qquad (4)$

Squaring both sides of (4): $13 - m^2 = m^2 + 10 - m^2 - 2m\sqrt{10-m^2}$

$\Rightarrow 2m\sqrt{10-m^2} = m^2 - 3$ $\hspace{4cm}$ (5)

Squaring both sides of (5): $4m^2(10-m^2) = (m^2-3)^2 \Rightarrow$

$40m^2 - 4m^4 = m^4 - 6m^2 + 9 \Rightarrow 5m^4 - 46m^2 + 9 = 0 \Rightarrow (5m^2-1)(m^2-9) = 0$.

So $m^2 = 9$ or $m^2 = \dfrac{1}{5}$ (ignored since $m^2 > 4$).

The answer is 9.

4.3. Triangle perimeter and area

Example 8. Find the perimeter of a right triangle whose hypotenuse is 2 and whose area is 1. Express your answer in simplest radical form.

Solution: $2 + 2\sqrt{2}$.

By the Pythagorean Theorem, we have $a^2 + b^2 = c^2$ $\hspace{3cm}$ (1)

We are given that $\dfrac{1}{2}ab = 1$ $\hspace{2cm} \Rightarrow \hspace{1cm} 2ab = 4$ $\hspace{2cm}$ (2)

(1) + (2): $(a+b)^2 = 4 + c^2$ $\hspace{1.5cm} \Rightarrow \hspace{1cm} (a+b)^2 = 8 \hspace{0.5cm} \Rightarrow \hspace{0.5cm} a+b = 2\sqrt{2}$

The perimeter is $2 + 2\sqrt{2}$.

Example 9. (2014 Mathcounts National Sprint 16) A right triangle has a hypotenuse of 10 m and a perimeter of 22 m. In square meters, what is the area of the triangle?

Solution: 11.

Let the sides be a, b, and c. c is the hypotenuse.

$a+b+c = 22 \Rightarrow \hspace{0.5cm} a+b+10 = 22 \hspace{1.5cm} \Rightarrow \hspace{1cm} a+b = 12$ $\hspace{1.5cm}$ (1)

By Pythagorean theorem, $a^2 + b^2 = c^2$ $\hspace{1.5cm} \Rightarrow \hspace{1cm} a^2 + b^2 = 100$ $\hspace{1.5cm}$ (2)

Squaring both sides of (1): $(a+b)^2 = 12^2 \Rightarrow a^2 + 2ab + b^2 = 144$ $\hspace{1.5cm}$ (3)

Substituting (2) into (3): $2ab = 44 \hspace{0.5cm} \Rightarrow \hspace{0.5cm} \dfrac{ab}{2} = \dfrac{44}{4} = 11$.

Example 10. (1998 Mathcounts State Target) The lengths of two sides of an
isosceles triangle are 10 centimeters and 12 centimeters. Find the number
of square centimeters in the positive difference between the greatest and least
possible areas for this triangle. Express your answer as a decimal to the nearest
hundredth.

Solution: 6.54.
Case I: Draw $BD \perp AC$. Triangle ABD is a right triangle and

$BD = \sqrt{12^2 - 5^2} = \sqrt{119}$.

The area of triangle ABD is $\dfrac{10 \times \sqrt{119}}{2} = 5\sqrt{119}$.

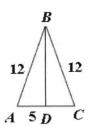

Case II: Draw $BD \perp AC$. Triangle ABD is a right triangle and

$BD = \sqrt{10^2 - 6^2} = 8$.

The area of triangle ABD is $\dfrac{12 \times 8}{2} = 48$.

The positive difference is $5\sqrt{119} - 48 \approx 6.54$.

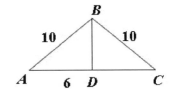

Example 11. (1994 Mathcounts National Sprint Problem 25) The perimeter of a
right triangle is 60 inches and the length of the altitude to the hypotenuse is 12
inches. How many square inches are in the area of the triangle?

Solution: 150.
Let a, b, and c be the three side lengths of the right triangle.
According to the problem, we have

$a + b + c = 60$ (1)

$a^2 + b^2 = c^2$ (2)

$\dfrac{a \times b}{2} = \dfrac{12 \times c}{2} \rightarrow ab = 12c$ (3)

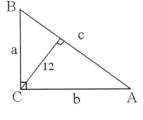

Method 1

(1) can be written as $a + b = 60 - c$ (4)

Squaring both sides of (4): $(a+b)^2 = (60-c)^2$ $\Rightarrow$

$a^2 + 2ab + b^2 = (60-c)^2 \Rightarrow$ $2ab + c^2 = (60-c)^2$ $\Rightarrow$

$2ab = (60-c)^2 - c^2$ $\Rightarrow$ $2ab = 3600 - 120c$ $\Rightarrow$

$2ab = 3600 - 10ab$

$\Rightarrow$ $12ab = 3600 \Rightarrow$ $\dfrac{ab}{2} = 150$.

Method 2.

Square both sides of (1) to get $a^2 + b^2 + c^2 + 2ab + 2bc + 2ac = 60^2$.

Substituting (2) and (3) into the above equation, we can obtain

$2c^2 + 2 \times 12c + 2cb + 2ca = 60^2$

$\Rightarrow 2c^2 + 2 \times 12c + 2c(b+a) = 60^2$

$\Rightarrow 2c^2 + 2 \times 12c + 2c(60-c) = 60^2$

$\Rightarrow 144c = 60^2$ $\Rightarrow 6c = 150$

The area of the triangle equals $\dfrac{12 \times c}{2} = 6c = 150$.

Example 12. The perimeter of triangle ABC is 24. M is the midpoint of AB such that $MC = MA = 5$. How many square inches are in the area of the triangle?

Solution: 24.

Since M is the midpoint of AB and $MA = 5$, $MB = 5$.

So $MA = MB = MC$. Thus $\angle ACB = 90°$.

So we have $AC + BC = 14$ (1)

and $AC^2 + BC^2 = 10^2$ (2)

Squaring both sides of (1): $AC^2 + 2AC \times BC + BC^2 = 14^2$ $\Rightarrow$

$2AC \times BC + 10^2 = 14^2$ $\Rightarrow$ $2AC \times BC = 14^2 - 10^2 = 96$.

$\Rightarrow$ $AC \times BC = 48$.

The area of the triangle is $S_{\triangle ABC} = \dfrac{AC \times BC}{2} = \dfrac{48}{2} = 24$.

Example 13. Find the perimeter of a right triangle whose hypotenuse is 2 and whose area is 2. Express your answer in simplest radical form.

Solution: $2 + 2\sqrt{3}$.
By the Pythagorean Theorem, we have $a^2 + b^2 = c^2$ (1)

We are given that $\frac{1}{2}ab = 2$ $\Rightarrow$ $2ab = 8$ (2)

(1) + (2): $(a+b)^2 = 8 + c^2$ $\Rightarrow$ $(a+b)^2 = 12$ $\Rightarrow$ $a+b = 2\sqrt{3}$
The perimeter is $2 + 2\sqrt{3}$.

Example 14. The lengths of three sides of a right triangle are all integers. One of the legs has the length 13. What is the perimeter of the triangle?

Solution: 182.

Let the other leg be x. the length of the hypotenuse is $\sqrt{x^2 + 13^2}$.

Since the length of the hypotenuse is an integer, we let $\sqrt{x^2 + 13^2} = k$
    $\Rightarrow x^2 + 13^2 = k^2$ $\Rightarrow k^2 - x^2 = 13^2$ $\Rightarrow (k-x)(k+x) = 13^2$.
We know that $k - x < k + x$.
So we have:
$k - x = 1$ (1)
$k + x = 13^2$ (2)
(1) + (2): $2k = 170$ $\Rightarrow$ $k = 85$.
Thus $x = 84$. The perimeter is $85 + 84 + 13 = 182$.

Example 15. (2008 Mathcounts National Team Problem 10) In the figure, what is the area of triangle ABD? Express your answer as a common fraction.

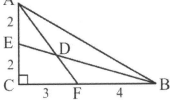

Solution: 56/11.
Connect CD and extend CD to meet AB at G as shown.
Since $AE = EC$, $S_{\triangle AED} = S_{\triangle CED} = a$.

$S_{\Delta ABD} = S_{\Delta CBD} = b + c = d + e.$

$S_{\Delta ACF} = 2a + b = 6$ (1)

$S_{\Delta ECB} = a + b + c = 7$ (2)

$\dfrac{S_{\Delta CFD}}{3} = \dfrac{S_{\Delta FBD}}{4} \Rightarrow \dfrac{b}{3} = \dfrac{c}{4}$ or $4b = 3c \Rightarrow c = \dfrac{4b}{3}$ (3)

Substituting (3) into (2): $a + b + \dfrac{4b}{3} = 7 \Rightarrow a + \dfrac{7b}{3} = 7$ (4)

(4) $\times 2 - (1)$: $b = \dfrac{24}{11}$.

Substituting the value of b into (3): $c = \dfrac{4b}{3} = \dfrac{4}{3} \times \dfrac{24}{11} = \dfrac{32}{11}$.

The answer is $b + c = \dfrac{24}{11} + \dfrac{32}{11} = \dfrac{56}{11}$.

4.4. Triangle side length

Example 16. Each triangle is a 30°-60°-90° triangle, and the hypotenuse of one triangle is the longer leg of an adjacent triangle. The hypotenuse of the largest triangle is 8 centimeters. What is the number of centimeters in the length of the longer leg of the smallest triangle? Express your answer as a common fraction.

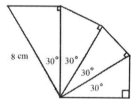

Solution: 9/2 (centimeters).

By (2.5), $BF = \dfrac{\sqrt{3}}{2} AF = 4\sqrt{3}$.

By (2.5), $FC = \dfrac{\sqrt{3}}{2} \times BF = 6$.

By (2.5), $FD = \dfrac{\sqrt{3}}{2} \times FC = \dfrac{\sqrt{3}}{2} \times 6 = 3\sqrt{3}$.

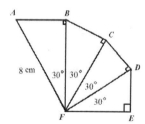

By (2.5), $FE = \dfrac{\sqrt{3}}{2} \times FD = \dfrac{\sqrt{3}}{2} \times 3\sqrt{3} = \dfrac{9}{2}$.

Example 17. Triangle ABC is shown with measures indicated. Find the value BC. Express your answer in simplest radical form.

Solution: $4\sqrt{2}$.

We draw the height from B to AC to meet AC at D.

$\triangle ABD$ is a 30-60-90 right triangle.

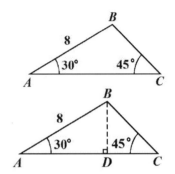

By Theorem 2, $BD = 4$.

$\triangle CBD$ is an isosceles right triangle. So $DC = 4$.

By Theorem 3, $BC = 4\sqrt{2}$.

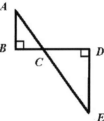

Example 18. (2000 State Sprint) In the diagram $BD = 6$ km, $AB = 3$ km, and $DE = 5$ km. What is the number of kilometers in AE?

Solution: 10.

Looking at the figure to the right and applying the Pythagorean Theorem to right triangle AFE gives us:

$AE^2 = AF^2 + FE^2$

$\Rightarrow \qquad AE = \sqrt{AF^2 + FE^2} = \sqrt{8^2 + 6^2} = 10$.

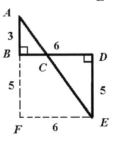

Example 19. (2014 Mathcounts National Sprint Problem 22) What is the smallest integer greater than 38 that cannot be the length of the hypotenuse of a right triangle with integer side lengths?

Solution: 42.

We know the following common Pythagorean triples: $(3n, 4n, 5n)$; $(5n, 12n, 13n)$; $(7n, 24n, 25n)$; $(8n, 15n, 17n)$; and $(9n, 40n, 41n)$.

So 39, 40, and 41 will all work. Now we like to find integer values of a and b such that $a^2 + b^2 = 42^2$ or we will say that 42 is our answer.
We know that for any Pythagorean Triple, one side is divisible by 3, another by 4, and another by 5. One side may have two of these divisors.

Since 42 is divisible by 3 (not by 4 or 5). So either a or b is divisible by 4. Let us say a is divisible 4. So b also must be even.
Let $a = 4m$, $b = 2n$. $a^2 + b^2 = 42^2$ becomes $(4m)^2 + (2n)^2 = 42^2 \Rightarrow$
$(2m)^2 + n^2 = 21^2$.
So $(2m)^2 = 21^2 - n^2$ and $21^2 - n^2$ must be an even perfect square number.
We know that $n^2 \equiv 1 \bmod 4$ $\qquad \Rightarrow n^2 \equiv 3^2 \qquad \bmod 4$
Thus all the possible values for n are: $n = 3, 7, 11, 15, 19$. None of these values leads $21^2 - n^2$ to be an even perfect square number. So 42 is our answer.

Example 20. Triangle ABC has sides AC, BC and AB measuring 18, 24 and 30 units, respectively. If D is the midpoint of segment AB, what is the length of segment CD?

Solution: 15.
Note that three sides of the triangle is a Pythagorean triple.
By Theorem 6, $CD = AD = DB = \dfrac{1}{2} AB = 15$.

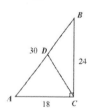

Example 21. A right triangle has the property that the lengths of its sides form a geometric progression, (i.e. the ratio of shorter leg to the longer leg is the same as the ratio of the longer leg to the hypotenuse.) What is the ratio of the hypotenuse to the shorter leg? Express your answer in simplest radical form.

Solution: $\dfrac{1+\sqrt{5}}{2}$.

Let three sides be a, b, and c. c is the hypotenuse.
We have

$$a^2 + b^2 = c^2 \qquad\qquad (1)$$

$$\dfrac{a}{b} = \dfrac{b}{c} \qquad\qquad \Rightarrow \qquad b^2 = ac \qquad\qquad (2)$$

Substituting (2) into (1): $a^2 + ac = c^2$ $\qquad\qquad (3)$

We divide each term of (3) by a^2: $1 + \dfrac{c}{a} = (\dfrac{c}{a})^2$ $\qquad\qquad (4)$

Let $m = \dfrac{c}{a}$, (4) becomes: $m^2 - m - 1 = 0$

$$\Rightarrow \qquad m = \dfrac{-(-1) \pm \sqrt{(-1)^2 - 4 \times 1 \times (-1)}}{2} = \dfrac{1+\sqrt{5}}{2} \quad (\dfrac{1-\sqrt{5}}{2} \text{ ignored}).$$

Example 22. A triangle has sides of lengths 14, 11, and 7. Find the length of the altitude of the triangle drawn to the longest side. Express your answer in simplest radical form.

Solution: $\dfrac{12\sqrt{10}}{7}$.

Method 1:
We draw the figure. Applying the Pythagorean Theorem to $\triangle ACD$:

$$AC^2 - AD^2 = CD^2 \qquad \Rightarrow \qquad 7^2 - x^2 = CD^2 \qquad (1)$$

Applying the Pythagorean Theorem to $\triangle BCD$:

$$BC^2 - DB^2 = CD^2 \qquad \Rightarrow \qquad 11^2 - (14-x)^2 = CD^2 \quad (2)$$

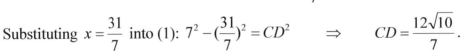

$$(1) - (2):\ 7^2 - x^2 = 11^2 - (14-x)^2 \qquad \Rightarrow \qquad x = \dfrac{31}{7}.$$

Substituting $x = \dfrac{31}{7}$ into (1): $7^2 - (\dfrac{31}{7})^2 = CD^2 \qquad \Rightarrow \qquad CD = \dfrac{12\sqrt{10}}{7}.$

Method 2:
The semi perimeter of the triangle is $(7 + 11 + 14)/2 = 16$.

By the Heron Formula, the area of the triangle is
$$\sqrt{16(16-7)(16-11)(16-14)} = 12\sqrt{10}.$$

Also the area can be calculated by $\frac{1}{2} \times 14 \times CD.$

So $\frac{1}{2} \times 14 \times CD = 12\sqrt{10}$ $\Rightarrow$ $CD = \frac{12\sqrt{10}}{7}.$

Example 23. In the right triangle ABC shown, E and D are the trisection points of the hypotenuse AB. If $CD = 7$ and $CE = 6$, what is the length of hypotenuse AB? Express your answer in simplest radical form.

Solution: $3\sqrt{17}$.

Draw $DG \parallel BC$, $EF \parallel AC$ as shown.

Since $AD = EB$, $\angle ADG = \angle EBF$, $\angle GAD = \angle FEB$, ΔADG is congruent to ΔEBF.

Let $AG = EF = x$ and $GD = BF = y$.
$CG = 2x$ and $CF = 2y$.

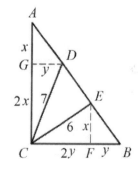

Applying Pythagorean Theorem to right triangle CDG :
$$(2x)^2 + y^2 = 7^2 \qquad (1)$$

Applying Pythagorean Theorem to right triangle CFE:
$$(2y)^2 + x^2 = 6^2 \qquad (2)$$

(1) + (2): $5x^2 + 5y^2 = 7^2 + 6^2 = 85 \Rightarrow x^2 + y^2 = 17$.

Thus $BE = \sqrt{x^2 + y^2} = \sqrt{17}$.

$AB = 3BE = 3\sqrt{17}$.

Example 24. (1992 Mathcounts State Sprint Problem 25) Right triangle ABC with right angle at vertex C has median AD of length 5 and median BE of length $2\sqrt{10}$. Find the length of the hypotenuse of triangle ABC. Express your answer in simplest radical form.

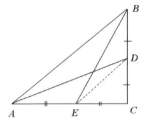

Solution: $2\sqrt{13}$.

Method 1:

Applying Pythagorean Theorem to right triangle ECB

: $BE^2 - EC^2 = BC^2$ (1)

Applying Pythagorean Theorem to right triangle ACB: $AD^2 - DC^2 = AC^2$ (2)

(1) + (2): $AC^2 + BC^2 = BE^2 + AD^2 - EC^2 - DC^2$

$= BE^2 + AD^2 - (\frac{1}{2}AC)^2 - (\frac{1}{2}BC)^2$

Or $AC^2 + BC^2 + \frac{1}{4}AC^2 + \frac{1}{4}BC^2 = BE^2 + AD^2 \Rightarrow \frac{5}{4}(AC^2 + BC^2) = BE^2 + AD^2$

$\Rightarrow \quad AB^2 = \frac{4}{5}(AD^2 + BE^2) = \frac{4}{5}[5^2 + (2\sqrt{10})^2] = \frac{4}{5}(65) = 52$.

$AB = \sqrt{52} = 2\sqrt{13}$.

Method 2:

Theorem: $\triangle ABC$ is a right triangle. If D and E are midpoints of BC and AC, respectively, then $4(AD^2 + BE^2) = 5AB^2$.

$AB^2 = \frac{4}{5}(AD^2 + BE^2) = \frac{4}{5}[5^2 + (2\sqrt{10})^2] = \frac{4}{5}(65) = 52$

$AB = \sqrt{52} = 2\sqrt{13}$.

Example 25. In triangle ABC, $BC = 30$, $AC = 20$. AD and BE are two medians on BC and AC, respectively with $AD \perp BE$. Find the length of AB. Express your answer in simplest radical form.

119

Solution: $2\sqrt{65}$.

Let the point of intersection of AD and BE be G.

G is the centroid of triangle ABC. Let $BE = 2n$, $AD = 3m$.

So $EG = n$, $BG = 2n$; $AG = 2m$, $DG = m$.

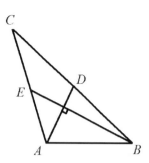

Applying Pythagorean Theorem to right triangle AGE :

$AG^2 + EG^2 = AE^2 \quad \Rightarrow \quad n^2 + (2m)^2 = 10^2 \qquad (1)$

Applying Pythagorean Theorem to right triangle BDG:

$BG^2 + DG^2 = BD^2 \quad \Rightarrow \quad (2n)^2 + n^2 = 15^2 \qquad (2)$

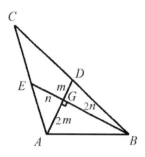

$(1) + (2): 5n^2 + 5m^2 = 10^2 + 15^2 \Rightarrow \quad n^2 + m^2 = 65 \quad (3)$

$(3) \times 4: 4n^2 + 4m^2 = 4 \times 65 \quad \Rightarrow$

$(2n)^2 + (2m)^2 = AB^2 = 4 \times 65 \Rightarrow AB = \sqrt{4 \times 65} = 2\sqrt{65}$.

Example 26. Given a right triangle ABC with $\angle A = 90°$, AD is the altitude from A to BC. Find AB/AC if $BD/DC = 1/4$. Express your answer as a common fraction.

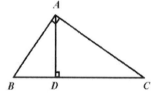

Solution: 1/2.

Method 1:

We know that $BD/DC = 1/4$. Let $BD = 1$. Then $DC = 4$.

We also know that $AD^2 = BD \times DC = 1 \times 4 = 4$. So $AD = 2$.

The Pythagorean Theorem applied to $\triangle ABD$ gives
$AB^2 = BD^2 + AD^2 = 2^2 + 1^2 = 5$ $\qquad\qquad$ (1)

The Pythagorean Theorem applied to $\triangle ADC$ gives
$AC^2 = DC^2 + AD^2 = 4^2 + 2^2 = 20$ $\qquad\qquad$ (2)

$(1) \div (2): \dfrac{AB}{AC} = \sqrt{\dfrac{5}{20}} = \dfrac{1}{2}$.

Method 2:

We know that $\triangle ABC \sim \triangle ACD \sim \triangle ABD$ and:

$$AC^2 = BC \times DC \qquad\qquad (1)$$
$$AB^2 = BC \times BD \qquad\qquad (2)$$

$$(2) \div (1): \quad \frac{AB^2}{AC^2} = \frac{BC \times BD}{BC \times DC} = \frac{BD}{DC} = \frac{1}{4} \qquad \Rightarrow \qquad \frac{AB}{AC} = \sqrt{\frac{1}{4}} = \frac{1}{2}.$$

5. PROBLEMS

Problem 1. In triangle ABC, $\angle C = 90°$. $AC = 6$, $BC = 8$. Find the area of the regions outside the circle but inside the triangle. Express the answer in terms of π.

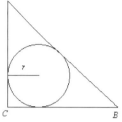

Problem 2. The two circles as shown have the same center C. Chord AD is tangent to the inner circle at B. Find the shaded area if $AD = 24$. Express the answer in terms of π.

Problem 3. As shown in the figure, $\angle B = 90°$, $AB = 3$, $BC = 4$, $CD = 13$, $AD = 12$. Find the area of quadrilateral $ABCD$.

Problem 4. The area of trapezoid $ABCD$ is 318 cm². The altitude is 12 cm, AB is 13 cm, and CD is 37 cm. What is BC, in centimeters? Express your answer as a common fraction.

Problem 5. Square $ABCD$ has sides of length 3. Segments CM and CN divide the square's area into three equal parts. How long is the segment connecting M and N? Express your answer in simplest radical form.

Problem 6. Consider a quadrilateral $ABCD$ with $AB = 4$, $BC = 10\sqrt{3}$ and $\angle DAB$ = 150°, $\angle ABC = 90°$, and $\angle BCD = 30°$. Find DC.

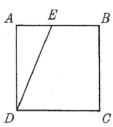

Problem 7. $ABCD$ is a rectangle and $DE = DC$. Given $AD = 5$ and $BE = 3$, find DE. Express your answer as a common fraction.

Problem 8. Right triangle ABC with $\angle B = 90°$, $AC = 2$, $AB + BC = \sqrt{6}$. Find the area of $\triangle ABC$. Express your answer as a common fraction.

Problem 9. A right triangle with integer side lengths a, b, and c satisfies $a < b < c$ and $a + c = 49$. What is the area of the right triangle?

Problem 10. (2000 National Sprint) In $\triangle ABC$, $\angle C$ is a right angle. Point M is the midpoint of $\overline{AB}$, point N is the midpoint of $\overline{AC}$, and point O is the midpoint of $\overline{AM}$. The perimeter of $\triangle ABC$ is 112 cm, and $ON = 12.5$ cm. What is the number of square centimeters in the area of quadrilateral $MNCB$?

Problem 11. The perimeter of a right triangle is $2 + \sqrt{6}$ inches and the length of the median to the hypotenuse is 1 inches. How many square inches are in the area of the triangle? Express your answer as a common fraction.

Problem 12. The length of one side of a triangle is 2 and the length of the median to this side is 1. Find the area of the triangle if the sum of the lengths of other two sides is $1 + \sqrt{3}$. Express your answer in simplest radical form.

Problem 13. The lengths of three sides of a right triangle are all integers. One of the legs has the length 11. What is the perimeter of the triangle?

Problem 14. An irregular hexagon *DEFMNL* is drawn as follows: We start with a right triangle *ABC*, draw the squares on the legs and hypotenuse, and then join in sequence the free vertices of the squares. If the hypotenuse of triangle ABC has length 13 and the triangle *ABC* has area 30, find the area of the hexagon *DEFMNL*.

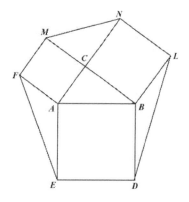

Problem 15. In the figure shown, $AB = BC = 1$ inch. $AD \mathbin{/\mkern-5mu/} BC$, $CD \mathbin{/\mkern-5mu/} AE$. What is the number of inches in the length of AE? Express your answer in simplest radical form.

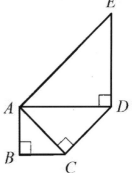

Problem 16. (1986 National Target) Find the length of AF. Express your answer in simplest radical form.

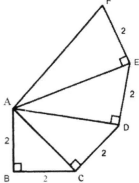

Problem 17. For what positive value of x is there a right triangle with sides $x + 1$, $4x$, and $4x + 1$?

Problem 18. (2001 Mathcounts National Team Problem 4) The rules for a race require that all runners start at A, touch any part of the 1200-meter wall, and stop at B. What is the number of meters in the minimum distance a participant must run? Express your answer to the nearest meter.

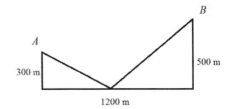

Problem 19. In triangle ABC, $\angle C = 90°$. $\angle 1 = \angle 2$. $CD = 15$ mm, $BD = 25$ mm. Find AC.

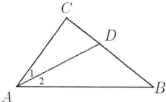

Problem 20. The sides of a right triangle have lengths $x - y$, x, and $x + y$ where $x > y > 0$. Find the ratio of x to y. Express your answer in the form $of\ a{:}b$.

A. $3 : 2$ B. $2 : 1$ C. $3 : 1$ D. $4 : 1$ E. $4 : 3$

Problem 21. In the acute triangle ABC, the line segments AD and BE are altitudes. If the length of AB is 10, the length of CD is 2, and the length of AD is 6, what is the length of BE? Express your answer in simplest radical form.

Problem 22. MK and LJ are the hypotenuses of overlapping right triangles KLM and JKL. $MK \perp LJ$, the length of MK is $6\sqrt{5}$, the length of LK is $6\sqrt{3}$. Find the length of JK. Express your answer in simplest radical form.

Problem 23. Given a right triangle with sides of length a, b, and c and area, $a^2 + b^2 - c^2$, find c/b, the ratio of the legs of the right triangle.

Problem 24. In triangle *ABC, BC* = 4, *AC* = 3 . *AD* and *BE* are two medians on *BC* and *AC*, respectively with *AD* ⊥ *BE*. Find the length of *AB*. Express your answer in simplest radical form.

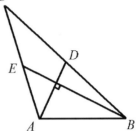

Problem 25. (2001 Mathcounts National Team Problem 9) The numbers $\sqrt{2u-1}$, $\sqrt{2u+1}$, and $2\sqrt{u}$ are the side lengths of a triangle. How many degrees are in the measure of the largest angle?

Problem 26. In a right triangle with integer side lengths, the shortest leg has length 17 units. What is the length of the hypotenuse, in units?

6. SOLUTIONS

Problem 1. Solution: $24 - 4\pi$.

Since $AC = 6$ and $BC = 8$, $AB = 10$.

By Theorem 4: $r = \dfrac{AC + BC - AB}{2} = \dfrac{6 + 8 - 10}{2} = 2$

The area of the circle is $\pi r^2 = 4\pi$

The area of the triangle is $\dfrac{AC \times BC}{2} = \dfrac{6 \times 8}{2} = 24$

The answer is $24 - 4\pi$.

Problem 2. Solution: B.

Connect AB. Draw $CB \perp AD$ at B.

We know that triangle ABC is a right triangle. Applying Pythagorean Theorem we get $AC^2 - BC^2 = AB^2$ $\qquad\qquad$ (1)

S, the shaded area = the area of the larger circle – the area of the smaller circle:

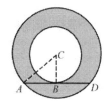

$S = \pi \times AC^2 - \pi \times BC^2 = \pi(AC^2 - BC^2)$ $\qquad$ (2)

 Substituting (1) into (2):

$S = \pi \times AB^2 = \pi \times 12^2 = 144\pi$.

Problem 3. Solution: 36.

$\triangle ACD$ is a right triangle and $\angle DAC = 90°$.

Area of $ABCD$ = Area of $\triangle ABC$ + Area of $\triangle ACD$

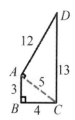

$\dfrac{1}{2} \times 3 \times 4 + \dfrac{1}{2} \times 12 \times 5 = 6 + 30 = 36$ square units.

Problem 4. Solution: 13/2.

Let E and F be the feet of the perpendicular from B and C to AD, respectively. Applying Pythagorean Theorem to right $\triangle ABE$, $AE^2 = AB^2 - BE^2 = 13^2 - 12^2 = 5^2$. So $AE = 5$.

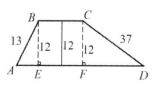

Applying Pythagorean Theorem to right ΔDCF,

$DF^2 = DC^2 - CF^2 = 37^2 - 12^2 = 35^2$. So $DF = 35$.

The trapezoid has area $\dfrac{BC + AD}{2} \times 12 = 318 \Rightarrow$ $BC + AE + EF + DF = 53$

$\Rightarrow$ $BC + 5 + BC + 35 = 53 \Rightarrow$ $BC = \dfrac{13}{2}$.

Problem 5. Solution: $\sqrt{2}$.

One-third of the square's area is 3, so triangle MBC has area $3 =$

$\dfrac{1}{2} \times MB \times BC$ $\Rightarrow$ $MB = 2$.

So $AM = AN = 1$.

Applying Pythagorean Theorem to right ΔAMN,

$MN^2 = AM^2 + AN^2 = 1^2 + 1^2 = 2$. So $MN = \sqrt{2}$.

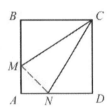

Problem 6. Solution: 17.

First we see that the angle D is $90° = 360° - 150° - 90° - 30°$.

Extend CD and BA to meet at E. We see that $\angle E = 60°$.

By Theorem 5 in $\Delta\ EBC$, $EB = 10$ and $EA = 6$.

By Theorem 5, in $\Delta\ EAD$, $ED = 3$.

Applying the Pythagorean Theorem to the right triangle

EBC: $BC^2 + EB^2 = EC^2 \Rightarrow (10\sqrt{3})^2 + 10^2 = (3 + DC)^2 \Rightarrow$

$DC = 17$.

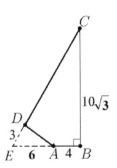

Problem 7. Solution: $\dfrac{17}{3}$.

$AE = AB - BE = DC - 3$.

ΔDAE is a right triangle. $DE^2 = AD^2 + AE^2$

Since $DE = DC$ and $AE = DC - 3$, we have $DC^2 = 5^2 + (DC - 3)^2$ $\Rightarrow$

$DC^2 = 5^2 + DC^2 - 6DC + 9$ $\Rightarrow$ $6DC = 5^2 + 9 = 34$ $\Rightarrow$ $DC = \dfrac{34}{6} = \dfrac{17}{3}$.

Problem 8. Solution: 1/2.

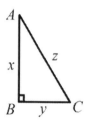

$(x + y)^2 = \left(\sqrt{6}\right)^2$ $\Rightarrow$ $x^2 + 2xy + y^2 = 6$

By the Pythagorean Theorem: $x^2 + y^2 = 4$

So $2xy = 2$ $\Rightarrow$ $\dfrac{xy}{2} = \dfrac{1}{2}$.

Problem 9. Solution: 210.

We have the following Pythagorean Triples:

a	b	c
20	21	29
12	35	37

The area of the right triangle is then $\dfrac{1}{2} \times 20 \times 21 = \dfrac{1}{2} \times 12 \times 35 = 210$.

Problem 10. Solution: 252.

Let $AC = x$ and $BC = y$.

We know that $MO = 12.5$ and $MB = 12.5 \times 2 = 25$.

$AB = 50$, so by the Pythagorean Theorem,

$x^2 + y^2 = 50^2$ (1)

The perimeter equals 112, so $x + y + 50 = 112$ (2)

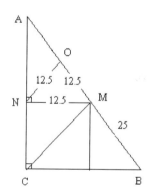

From (2), we get: $x + y = 62$ or $(x + y)^2 = 62^2$

Or $x^2 + 2xy + y^2 = 62^2$ (3)

(3) – (1) gives: $2xy = 62^2 - 50^2$

$\dfrac{xy}{2} = \dfrac{(60 - 50)(60 + 50)}{4} = \dfrac{12 \times 112}{4} = 336$.

$S_{\triangle ANM} = \dfrac{1}{4} S_{\triangle ABC}$, so $S_{BCNM} = \dfrac{3}{4} S_{\triangle ABC} = \dfrac{3}{4} \times 336 = 252$.

Problem 11. Solution: $\dfrac{1}{2}$.

Let a, b, and c be the three side lengths of the right triangle.
By the Pythagorean Theorem, we have $a^2 + b^2 = c^2$ (1)

$a + b + c = 2 + \sqrt{6}$ (2)

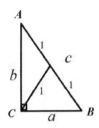

We know that $c = 2$. So (1) becomes $a + b + c = \sqrt{6}$ (3)

Squaring both sides of (4): $(a+b)^2 = 6$ $\Rightarrow$ $ab = 1$

$S_{\triangle ABC} = \dfrac{a \times b}{2} = \dfrac{1}{2}$.

Problem 12. Solution: $\dfrac{\sqrt{3}}{2}$.

Since the median is 1, and the side length is 2, this triangle is a right triangle.
Let a, b, and c be the three side lengths of the right triangle.
By the Pythagorean Theorem, we have $a^2 + b^2 = 2^2$ (1)

$a + b = 1 + \sqrt{3}$ (2)

Squaring both sides of (2): $(a+b)^2 = (1+\sqrt{3})^2 \Rightarrow a^2 + 2ab + b^2 = 4 + 2\sqrt{3}$ (3)

Substituting (1) into (3): $4 + 2ab = 4 + 2\sqrt{3}$ $\Rightarrow$ $2ab = 2\sqrt{3}$ $\Rightarrow$ $ab = \sqrt{3}$.

$S_{\triangle ABC} = \dfrac{a \times b}{2} = \dfrac{\sqrt{3}}{2}$.

Problem 13. Solution: 132.

Let the other leg be x. the length of the hypotenuse is $\sqrt{x^2 + 11^2}$.

Since the length of the hypotenuse is an integer, we let $\sqrt{x^2 + 11^2} = k$

$\Rightarrow x^2 + 11^2 = k^2$ $\Rightarrow k^2 - x^2 = 11^2$ $\Rightarrow (k-x)(k+x) = 11^2$.

We know that $k - x < k + x$.

So we have:

$k - x = 1$ (1)

$k + x = 11^2$ (2)

(1) + (2): $2k = 122$ $\Rightarrow$ $k = 61$.

Thus $x = 60$. The perimeter is $61 + 60 + 11 = 132$.

Problem 14. Solution: 458.
As shown in the figure, four triangles have the same
area and $S_1 = S_2 + S_3$.
The answer is $30 \times 4 + 13^2 \times 2 = 458$.

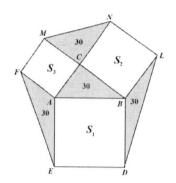

Problem 15. Solution: $2\sqrt{2}$ (inches).
All triangles are $45° - 90° - 45°$ right triangles.
By **Theorem 3**, $AC = \sqrt{2} \times AB = 2$. $AD = \sqrt{2} \times AC = 2$. $AE = \sqrt{2} \times AD = 2\sqrt{2}$.

Problem 16. Solution: $2\sqrt{5}$.
$AB^2 + BC^2 = AC^2 \qquad \Rightarrow AC^2 = 2^2 + 2^2 = 8$.
$AD^2 = AC^2 + CD^2 = 8 + 2^2 = 12$.
$AE^2 = AD^2 + ED^2 = 12 + 2^2 = 16$.
$AF^2 = AE^2 + EF^2 = 16 + 2^2 = 20 \qquad \Rightarrow \qquad AF = 2\sqrt{5}$.

Problem 17. Solution: 6.
Let the hypotenuse be $4x + 1$.
By the Pythagorean Theorem, $(x + 1)^2 + (4x)^2 = (4x + 1)^2 \quad \Rightarrow \quad x = 6\ (x = 0$
ignored).

Problem 18. Solution: 1442 (meters).
We reflect point A over EF. Connect CB to meet
EF at g. Extend BF to D such that $FD = EC$. We
see that $CD = EF = 1200$ and $BD = 500 + 300 = 800$.
Applying the Pythagorean Theorem to right
triangle BCD:

$$BC^2 = CD^2 + BD^2 \qquad \Rightarrow \qquad BC = \sqrt{1200^2 + 800^2} = 400\sqrt{13} \approx 1442.$$

Problem 19. Solution: 30.

Method 1: By the angle bisector theorem, we have:

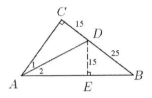

$$\frac{AC}{CD} = \frac{AB}{BD} \qquad \Rightarrow \qquad \frac{AC}{15} = \frac{AB}{25}$$

$$AB = \frac{AC}{15} \times 25 = \frac{5}{3} AC .$$

$\angle C = 90°$. By the Pythagorean Theorem:

$$AC^2 + BC^2 = AB^2 \qquad \Rightarrow \qquad AB^2 - AC^2 = BC^2$$

$$\Rightarrow \left(\frac{5}{3} AC\right)^2 - AC^2 = (15 + 25)^2 \Rightarrow \quad \frac{16}{9} AC^2 = 40^2 \Rightarrow \qquad AC = 30.$$

Method 2:

Draw $DE \perp AB$ and meets AB at E. $\triangle CAD$ and $\triangle AED$ are congruent. $DE = CD = 15$ mm. $\triangle DBE$ is a $15 - 20 - 25$ right triangle and is similar to $\triangle ABC$.

$$\frac{AC}{CB} = \frac{DE}{EB} \qquad \Rightarrow \qquad \frac{AC}{15 + 25} = \frac{15}{25} \qquad \Rightarrow \qquad AC = 30.$$

Problem 20. Solution: $4 : 1$.

Since $x > y > 0$, $x + y$ is the longest side.

So we have $\qquad (x + y)^2 = x^2 + (x - y)^2$ \hfill (1)

Dividing both sides of (1) by y^2: $(\frac{x}{y} + 1)^2 = (\frac{x}{y})^2 + (\frac{x}{y} - 1)^2$ \hfill (2)

Let $m = \frac{x}{y}$. (2) becomes: $(m + 1)^2 = m^2 + (m - 1)^2 \quad \Rightarrow \quad m^2 = 4m \quad \Rightarrow \quad m = 4$.

$$\frac{x}{y} = m = \frac{4}{1} .$$

Problem 21. Solution: $3\sqrt{10}$.

Applying the Pythagorean Theorem to $\triangle ACD$:

$$AD^2 + CD^2 = AC^2 \qquad \Rightarrow \qquad 6^2 + 2^2 = AC^2 \Rightarrow$$
$$AC = 2\sqrt{10} .$$

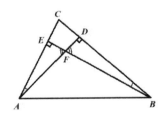

$\triangle ADB$ is a 6–8–10 right triangle. So $DB = 8$.

We also see from the figure that $\angle EAF + \angle F = \angle DBF + \angle F = 90°$. So $\angle EAF = \angle DBF$. Thus $\triangle BCE$ is similar to $\triangle ACD$ and $\dfrac{AC}{BC} = \dfrac{AD}{BE}$ $\Rightarrow$

$$\frac{2\sqrt{10}}{10} = \frac{6}{BE} \Rightarrow \qquad BE = 3\sqrt{10}\,.$$

Problem 22. Solution: $9\sqrt{2}$.

Applying the Pythagorean Theorem to $\triangle KLM$:

$ML^2 + KL^2 = MK^2 \Rightarrow ML^2 = (6\sqrt{5})^2 - (6\sqrt{3})^2 \Rightarrow ML = 6\sqrt{2}$.

We know that $\triangle KLM$ is similar to $\triangle JKL$.

So $\dfrac{ML}{KL} = \dfrac{KL}{JK} \Rightarrow \dfrac{6\sqrt{2}}{6\sqrt{3}} = \dfrac{6\sqrt{3}}{JK}$

$\Rightarrow JK = \dfrac{18}{\sqrt{2}} = 9\sqrt{2}$.

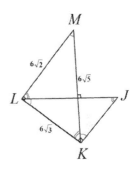

Problem 23. Solution: 4.

By the Pythagorean Theorem, we have $b^2 + c^2 = a^2$ $\qquad$ (1)

We are given that $\dfrac{1}{2}bc = a^2 + b^2 - c^2 \Rightarrow bc = 2a^2 + 2b^2 - 2c^2$ (2)

Substituting (1) into (2): $4b = c$ $\qquad \Rightarrow \qquad c/b = 4$.

Problem 24. Solution: $\sqrt{5}$.

Let the point of intersection of AD and BE be G.

G is the centroid of triangle ABC. Let $BE = 2n$, $AD = 3m$.

So $EG = n$, $BG = 2n$; $AG = 2m$, $DG = m$.

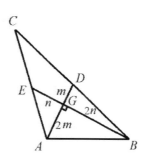

Applying Pythagorean Theorem to right triangle AGE :

$AG^2 + EG^2 = AE^2 \qquad \Rightarrow \qquad n^2 + (2m)^2 = (\dfrac{3}{2})^2 \qquad$ (1)

Applying Pythagorean Theorem to right triangle BDG: $BG^2 + DG^2 = BD^2$

$$\Rightarrow \quad (2n)^2 + n^2 = (\frac{4}{2})^2 \quad (2)$$

$(1) + (2)$: $5n^2 + 5m^2 = \dfrac{9}{4} + 4 = \dfrac{25}{4} \Rightarrow n^2 + m^2 = \dfrac{5}{4}$ $\quad (3)$

$(3) \times 4$: $4n^2 + 4m^2 = 4 \times \dfrac{5}{4} = 5 \qquad \Rightarrow (2n)^2 + (2m)^2 = AB^2 = 5 \Rightarrow AB = \sqrt{5}$.

Problem 25. Solution: 90°.

We see that $(\sqrt{2u-1})^2 + (\sqrt{2u+1})^2 = (2\sqrt{u})^2$. So this is a right triangle and the largest angle measures 90°.

Problem 26. Solution: 145.

Let the other leg be b and the hypotenuse be c.

$c^2 - b^2 = 17^2 \qquad \Rightarrow \qquad (c-b)(c+b) = 17^2$.

We know that $c - b < c + b$.

So we have:

$c - b = 1$ $\qquad\qquad\qquad\qquad$ (1)

$c + b = 17^2$ $\qquad\qquad\qquad\quad$ (2)

$(1) + (2)$: $2c = 290 \qquad \Rightarrow \qquad c = 145$.

BASIC KNOWLEDGE

1. Vieta's Theorem

If x_1 and x_2 are two roots of a quadratic equation $ax^2 + bx + c = 0$, $(a \neq 0)$, then

$$x_1 + x_2 = -\frac{b}{a} \tag{1.1}$$

$$x_1 \cdot x_2 = \frac{c}{a} \tag{1.2}$$

Proof:
Let x_1 and x_2 be the two roots of a quadratic equation
$ax^2 + bx + c = 0$, $(a \neq 0)$.

$$x_1 = \frac{-b + \sqrt{b^2 - 4ac}}{2a}, \quad x_2 = \frac{-b - \sqrt{b^2 - 4ac}}{2a}.$$

The sum of x_1 and x_2 is obtained by adding the two equations together:

$$x_1 + x_2 = \frac{-b + \sqrt{b^2 - 4ac}}{2a} + \frac{-b - \sqrt{b^2 - 4ac}}{2a} = \frac{-2b}{2a} = -\frac{b}{a}.$$

The product of x_1 and x_2 is obtained by multiplying the two equations together:

$$x_1 \cdot x_2 = \frac{-b + \sqrt{b^2 - 4ac}}{2a} \cdot \frac{-b - \sqrt{b^2 - 4ac}}{2a} = \frac{(-b)^2 - (\sqrt{b^2 - 4ac})^2}{4a^2} = \frac{4ac}{4a^2} = \frac{c}{a}.$$

Note: When we derived Vieta's Theorem, the roots could have been real or not. However, if there is a problem stating that the roots are real (or positive), you must consider $\Delta \geq 0$ and $a \neq 0$. If it is necessary, you need to check if $\Delta \geq 0$ or not.

2. Useful Forms Of Vieta's Theorem

$$x_1^2 + x_2^2 = (x_1 + x_2)^2 - 2x_1x_2 \tag{2.1}$$

$$x_1^2 + x_2^2 = \frac{-b(x_1 + x_2) - 2c}{a} \tag{2.2}$$

$$x_1^2 + x_2^2 = \frac{b^2 - 2ac}{a^2} \tag{2.3}$$

$$x_1^3 + x_2^3 = (x_1 + x_2)[(x_1 + x_2)^2 - 3x_1x_2] \tag{2.4}$$

$$x_1^3 + x_2^3 = \frac{-b(x_1^2 + x_2^2) - c(x_1 + x_2)}{a} \tag{2.5}$$

$$x_1^3 + x_2^3 = \frac{3abc - b^3}{a^3} \tag{2.6}$$

$$x_1^n + x_2^n = \frac{-b(x_1^{n-1} + x_2^{n-1}) - c(x_1^{n-2} + x_2^{n-2})}{a} \tag{2.7}$$

$$(x_1 - x_2)^2 = (x_1 + x_2)^2 - 4x_1x_2 \tag{2.8}$$

$$\sqrt{x_1} + \sqrt{x_2} = \sqrt{x_1 + x_2 + 2\sqrt{x_1x_2}} \qquad (x_1 \geq 0, x_2 \geq 0) \tag{2.9}$$

$$\frac{1}{x_1} + \frac{1}{x_2} = \frac{x_1 + x_2}{x_1x_2} = -\frac{b}{a} \cdot \frac{a}{c} = -\frac{b}{c} \tag{2.10}$$

$$\frac{1}{x_1^2} + \frac{1}{x_2^2} = \frac{-b(\frac{1}{x_1} + \frac{1}{x_2}) - 2a}{c} = \frac{-b(-\frac{b}{c}) - 2a}{c} = \frac{b^2 - 2ac}{c^2} \tag{2.11}$$

$$\frac{1}{x_1^3} + \frac{1}{x_2^3} = \frac{-b^3 + 3abc}{c^3} \tag{2.12}$$

$$(\frac{1}{x_1})^3 + (\frac{1}{x_2})^3 = -\frac{b[(\frac{1}{x_1})^2 + (\frac{1}{x_2})^2] + a(\frac{1}{x_1} + \frac{1}{x_2})}{c} \tag{2.13}$$

In all the above formulas, x_1 and x_2 represent the two roots of the quadratic equation $ax^2 + bx + c = 0$.

3. Converse Of Vieta's Theorem

If x_1 and x_2 satisfy the following:

$$x_1 + x_2 = -\frac{b}{a}, \text{ and } x_1 \cdot x_2 = \frac{c}{a}$$

then x_1 and x_2 are two roots of a quadratic equation $ax^2 + bx + c = 0$, $(a \neq 0)$.

This theorem can be used to construct a quadratic equation.

Proof:

$$ax^2 + bx + c = a[x^2 + \frac{b}{a}x + \frac{c}{a}]$$

Since $\frac{b}{a} = -(x_1 + x_2)$, $x_1 \cdot x_2 = \frac{c}{a}$.

$$\therefore \quad ax^2 + bx + c = a[x^2 + \frac{b}{a}x + \frac{c}{a}] = a[x^2 - (x_1 + x_2)x + x_1 x_2]$$

Substituting x_1 for x into the left hand side of the above equation:

$$ax_1^2 + bx_1 + c = a[x_1^2 - (x_1 + x_2)x_1 + x_1 x_2] = a[x_1^2 - x_1^2 - x_1 x_2 + x_1 x_2] = 0.$$

So x_1 is the root of $ax^2 + bx + c = 0$.
Similarly, we have $ax_2^2 + bx_2 + c = a[x_2^2 - x_2^2 - x_1 x_2 + x_1 x_2] = 0$.
So x_2 is also the root of $ax^2 + bx + c = 0$.

4. Generalized Vieta's Theorem:

(1). Let x_1, x_2, and x_3 be the roots for a 3-degree polynomial
$a_0 x^3 + a_1 x^2 + a_2 x^1 + a_3 = 0$.
Then

$$x_1 + x_2 + x_3 = -\frac{a_1}{a_0} \tag{4.1}$$

$$x_1x_2 + x_2x_3 + x_3x_1 = \frac{a_2}{a_0} \qquad (4.2)$$

$$x_1x_2x_3 = -\frac{a_3}{a_0} \qquad (4.3)$$

(2). Let x_1, x_2, x_3, and x_4 be the roots for a 4-degree polynomial
$a_0x^4 + a_1x^3 + a_2x^2 + a_3x^1 + a_4 = 0$.
Then

$$x_1 + x_2 + x_3 + x_4 = -\frac{a_1}{a_0} \qquad (4.4)$$

$$x_1x_2 + x_1x_3 + x_1x_4 + x_2x_3 + x_2x_4 + x_3x_4 = \frac{a_2}{a_0} \qquad (4.5)$$

$$x_1x_2x_3 + x_1x_2x_4 + x_1x_3x_4 + x_2x_3x_4 = -\frac{a_3}{a_0} \qquad (4.6)$$

$$x_1x_2x_3x_4 = \frac{a_4}{a_0} \qquad (4.7)$$

5. A Different Form of Vieta Theorem

$$|x_2 - x_1| = \frac{\sqrt{b^2 - 4ac}}{|a|} \qquad (5.1)$$

If $a > 0$, then (1) can be simplified as

$$x_2 - x_1 = \frac{\sqrt{b^2 - 4ac}}{a} = \frac{\sqrt{\Delta}}{a} \qquad (5.2)$$

Proof:
According to Vieta's Theorem, we have

$$(x_2 - x_1)^2 = (x_1 + x_2)^2 - 4x_1x_2 = (-\frac{b}{a})^2 - 4\frac{c}{a} = \frac{b^2 - 4ac}{a^2}.$$

Hence: $\left| x_1 - x_2 \right| = \dfrac{\sqrt{b^2 - 4ac}}{|a|} = \dfrac{\sqrt{\Delta}}{|a|}$.

$$\left| x_1 - x_2 \right| = \left| \dfrac{-b + \sqrt{b^2 - 4ac}}{2a} - \dfrac{-b - \sqrt{b^2 - 4ac}}{2a} \right| = \dfrac{\sqrt{b^2 - 4ac}}{|a|} .$$

6. Signs of Two Real Roots

If x_1 and x_2 are real, the following rules are true:

$\Delta \geq 0$, $\dfrac{c}{a} > 0$, $\dfrac{b}{a} < 0$ $\Rightarrow$ both x_1 and x_2 are positive.

$\Delta \geq 0$, $\dfrac{c}{a} > 0$, $\dfrac{b}{a} > 0$ $\Rightarrow$ both x_1 and x_2 are negative.

$\Delta > 0$, $\dfrac{c}{a} < 0$ or $ac < 0$ $\Rightarrow$ x_1 and x_2 have opposite signs (one is positive and one is negative.

2. APPLICATIONS OF VIETA'S THEOREM

Example 1. What is the sum of the solutions of $6x^2 + 5x - 4 = 0$? Express your answer as a common fraction.

Solution: $- 5/6$.
By Vieta's Theorem, the sum of the solutions is $- 5/6$.

Example 2. If 2 is a root of $4x^2 - 11x + 6 = 0$, find the second root. Express your answer as a common fraction.

Solution: $\dfrac{3}{4}$

Method 1:
Let x_1 be the unknown, second root.

Using Vieta's Theorem, the product of the two roots is equal to

$$2 \cdot x_1 = \frac{6}{4} \implies x_1 = \frac{3}{4}.$$

Method 2:

Let x_1 be the unknown root. Using Vieta's Theorem, the sum of the two roots is

equal to $x_1 + 2 = \frac{11}{4} \implies x_1 = \frac{3}{4}.$

Example 3. The square of the difference of two roots of the equation $x^2 - 2x + q = 0$ is 16. What is the value for q?

Solution: -3.

Let x_1 and x_2 be the two roots.

By Vieta's Theorem, $x_1 + x_2 = -(-2) = 2$ and $x_1 x_2 = q$.

$(x_1 - x_2)^2 = (x_1 + x_2)^2 - 4x_1 x_2 = 16$.

So $2^2 - 4q = 16 \implies q = -3$.

Example 4. What is the sum of the reciprocals of the solutions of $4x^2 - 13x + 3 = 0$? Express your answer as a common fraction.

Solution: $\dfrac{13}{3}$.

Applying the Vieta's Theorem:

$$\frac{1}{r} + \frac{1}{s} = \frac{s+r}{rs} = \frac{-(\frac{-13}{4})}{\frac{3}{4}} = \frac{13}{3}$$

Example 5. If r and s are the solutions of $x^2 + 6x - 2 = 0$, what is the value of $r^3 + s^3$?

Solution: -252.

Method 1:

$r^3 + s^3 = (r+s)[(r+s)^2 - 3rs] = (-6)[(-6)^2 - 3(-2)] = -252$.

Method 2:

$r^3 + s^3 = \dfrac{3abc - b^3}{a^3} = \dfrac{3 \times 1 \times 6 \times (-2) - 6^3}{1^3} = -252$.

Example 6. Find $\dfrac{1}{\alpha^3} + \dfrac{1}{\beta^3}$ if α and β are two roots of the equation

$2x^2 + 5x - 3 = 0$. Express your answer as a mixed number.

Solution: $7\dfrac{26}{27}$.

Method 1:

By Vieta's Theorem, the sum and product of the two roots of the quadratic equals

$\alpha + \beta = -\dfrac{5}{2}$, $\alpha \cdot \beta = -\dfrac{3}{2}$.

We also know by (2.13) that $\left(\dfrac{1}{x_1}\right)^3 + \left(\dfrac{1}{x_2}\right)^3 = -\dfrac{b\left[\left(\dfrac{1}{x_1}\right)^2 + \left(\dfrac{1}{x_2}\right)^2\right] + a\left(\dfrac{1}{x_1} + \dfrac{1}{x_2}\right)}{c}$.

Since $\dfrac{1}{\alpha} + \dfrac{1}{\beta} = -\dfrac{b}{c} = +\dfrac{5}{3}$,

$\left(\dfrac{1}{\alpha}\right)^2 + \left(\dfrac{1}{\beta}\right)^2 = \left(\dfrac{1}{\alpha} + \dfrac{1}{\beta}\right)^2 - 2\dfrac{1}{\alpha} \cdot \dfrac{1}{\beta} = \left(+\dfrac{5}{3}\right)^2 - 2\left(-\dfrac{2}{3}\right) = \dfrac{37}{9}$

$\therefore \quad \left(\dfrac{1}{\alpha}\right)^3 + \left(\dfrac{1}{\beta}\right)^3 = -\dfrac{5 \cdot \dfrac{37}{9} + 2 \cdot \dfrac{5}{3}}{-3} = \dfrac{215}{27} = 7\dfrac{26}{27}$.

Method 2:

We know that $a = 2$, $b = 5$ and $c = -3$.

We also know by (2.12) that $\dfrac{1}{x_1^3} + \dfrac{1}{x_2^3} = \dfrac{-b^3 + 3abc}{c^3}$.

Therefore, $\dfrac{1}{\alpha^3} + \dfrac{1}{\beta^3} = $

$\dfrac{-b^3 + 3abc}{c^3} = \dfrac{-5^3 + 3 \times 2 \times 5 \times (-3)}{(-3)^3} = \dfrac{-125 - 90}{-27} = \dfrac{215}{27} = 7\dfrac{26}{27}$

Example 7. Find $\dfrac{b}{a^2} + \dfrac{a}{b^2}$ if $a \neq b, a^2 - 3a = 1$, and $b^2 - 3b = 1$.

Solution: 36.

Since $a^2 - 3a = 1$ can be written as $a^2 - 3a - 1 = 0$ and $b^2 - 3b = 1$ can be written as $b^2 - 3b - 1 = 0$, we know that a and b are two roots of the quadratic equation $x^2 - 3x - 1 = 0$. The discriminate of this quadratic equation $\Delta = (-3)^2 - 4 \times (-1) = 13 > 0$, so the two roots are also real.

Hence, by Vieta's Theorem, $a + b = 3$ and $ab = -1$.

Therefore, $\dfrac{b}{a^2} + \dfrac{a}{b^2} = \dfrac{a^3 + b^3}{(ab)^2} = a^3 + b^3 = (a + b)(a^2 - ab + b^2)$

$= (a + b)[(a + b)^2 - 3ab] = 3(3^2 + 3) = 36$.

Example 8. If the sum of the squares of two real roots of the equation

$2x^2 + ax - 2a + 1 = 0$ is $7\dfrac{1}{4}$, find the value of a.

Solution: 3.

Let the two roots be r and s.

By Vieta's Theorem, $r + s = -\dfrac{a}{2}$, and $rs = \dfrac{-2a + 1}{2}$.

So $r^2 + s^2 = (r+s)^2 - 2rs = \left(-\dfrac{a}{2}\right)^2 - 2 \times \dfrac{-2a+1}{2} = \dfrac{1}{4}(a^2 + 8a - 4)$.

$\dfrac{1}{4}(a^2 + 8a - 4) = 7\dfrac{1}{4}$ $\Rightarrow$ $\quad (a+11)(a-3) = 0$.

We get $a = -11$ or $a = 3$.

When $a = -11$, $\Delta = a^2 - 8(-2a+1) = (-11)^2 - 8[-2 \times (-11) + 1] < 0$. The equation has no real solutions.

So the answer is 3.

Example 9. If a and b are two roots of $x^2 + (m-2)x + 1 = 0$, find the value of $(1 + ma + a^2)(1 + mb + b^2)$.

Solution: 4.

Since both a and b are two roots of $x^2 + (m-2)x + 1 = 0$, we have

$a^2 + (m-2)a + 1 = 0$, and $b^2 + (m-2)b + 1 = 0$.

Or $\quad a^2 + ma + 1 = 2a$ $\hspace{3cm}$ (1)

and $\quad b^2 + mb + 1 = 2b$ $\hspace{3cm}$ (2)

(1) $\times$ (2): $(1 + ma + a^2)(1 + mb + b^2) = 4ab$.

By Vieta's Theorem, $ab = 1$.

Thus $(1 + ma + a^2)(1 + mb + b^2) = 4$.

Example 10. If a and b are two roots of $x^2 - x - 1 = 0$, find the value of $a^4 + 3b$.

Solution: 5.

Method 1:

By Vieta's Theorem, $a + b = 1$.

Since a is the root of $x^2 - x - 1 = 0$, $a^2 - a - 1 = 0$.

$a^4 + 3b = a^4 + 3(1 - a) = a^4 - 3a + 3$

$$= a^2(a^2 - a - 1) + a(a^2 - a - 1) + 2(a^2 - a - 1) + 5 = 5.$$

Method 2:

By Vieta's Theorem, $a + b = 1$.

Since a is the root of $x^2 - x - 1 = 0$, $a^2 - a - 1 = 0$ $\Rightarrow$ $a^2 = a + 1$.

$$a^4 + 3b = (a+1)^2 + 3b = a^2 + 2a + 1 + 3b$$
$$= (a+1) + 2a + 1 + 3b = 3(a+b) + 2 = 3 + 2 = 5.$$

Example 11. (2012 Mathcounts Handbook Problem 256) The solutions $x = u$ and $x = v$ of the quadratic equation $rx^2 + sx + t = 0$ are reciprocals of the solutions of the quadratic equation $(2 + a)x^2 + 5x + (2 - a) = 0$ for some integer a. If the *GCF* of r, s and t is 1, what is the value of $r + s + t$?

Solution: 9.

Method 1:

By the Vieta's Theorem,

$$u + v = -\frac{s}{r} \tag{1}$$

$$uv = \frac{t}{r} \tag{2}$$

$$\frac{1}{u} + \frac{1}{v} = -\frac{5}{2+a} \qquad \Rightarrow \qquad \frac{u+v}{uv} = -\frac{5}{2+a} \tag{3}$$

$$\frac{1}{uv} = \frac{2-a}{2+a} \tag{4}$$

Substituting (1) and (2) into (3) and (1) to (4):

$$\frac{u+v}{uv} = -\frac{5}{2+a} = \frac{-\dfrac{s}{r}}{\dfrac{t}{r}} = -\frac{s}{t} \qquad \Rightarrow \qquad \frac{5}{2+a} = \frac{s}{t} \tag{5}$$

$$\frac{2-a}{2+a} = \frac{r}{t} \tag{6}$$

$(5) \div (6)$: $\dfrac{5}{2+a} = \dfrac{s}{r}$ $\Rightarrow$ $5r = 2s - as$ $\Rightarrow$ $a = 2 - \dfrac{5r}{s}$ (7)

We know that a is an integer and r and s are relatively prime, so s must be 5.
Then $a = 2 - r$ or $r = 2 - a$ (8)

Substituting $s = 5$ into (5): $\dfrac{5}{2+a} = \dfrac{5}{t}$ $\Rightarrow$ $t = 2 + a$

$r + s + t = 2 - a + 5 + 2 + a = 9.$

Method 2:
Since u and v are the two solutions of the quadratic equation $rx^2 + sx + t = 0$, we have
$$ru^2 + su + t = 0 \qquad\qquad (1)$$

Since $1/u$ and $1/v$ are the two solutions of the quadratic equation $(2 + a)x^2 + 5x + (2 - a) = 0$, we have

$(2+a)(\dfrac{1}{u})^2 + 5\dfrac{1}{u} + (2-a) = 0$ $\Rightarrow$ $(2-a)u^2 + 5u + (2+a) = 0$ (2)

Comparing the coefficients of 1) and (2), we get:
$2 - a = r$
$s = 5$
$t = 2 + a$
$r + s + t = 2 - a + 5 + 2 + a = 9.$

Example 12. (1970 AMC) Consider $x^2 + px + q = 0$, where p and q are positive numbers. If the roots of this equation differ by 1, then p equals

(A) $\sqrt{4q+1}$ (B) $q-1$ (C) $-\sqrt{4q+1}$ (D) $q+1$ (E) $\sqrt{4q-1}$

Solution: A.
Method 1 (Official solution):

Call the roots r and $r+1$. Their sum is $-p = 2r+1$ and their product is $q = r(r+1)$. Thus

$$r = \frac{-p-1}{2}, \quad r+1 = \frac{-p+1}{2},$$

and

$$q = r(r+1) = \frac{(-p-1)(-p+1)}{2\cdot 2} = \frac{p^2-1}{4};$$

$p^2 = 4q+1$, and $p = \sqrt{4q+1}$.

Method 2 (our solution):

Let α and β be the two roots of the equation.

By Vieta's Theorem:

$\alpha + \beta = -p$ (1)

$\alpha\beta = q$ (2)

$|\alpha - \beta| = 1$ (3)

Squaring both sides of (3):

$|\alpha - \beta|^2 = 1 \quad \Rightarrow \quad \alpha^2 - 2\alpha\beta + \beta^2 = 1 \quad \Rightarrow \quad (\alpha + \beta)^2 - 4\alpha\beta = 1$ (4)

Substituting (1) and (2) into (4): $(-p)^2 - 4q = 1 \quad \Rightarrow \quad p^2 = 4q+1$.

Since p is positive, $p = \sqrt{4q+1}$.

Method 3 (our solution):

$$x_2 - x_1 = \frac{\sqrt{b^2 - 4ac}}{a} = \frac{\sqrt{\Delta}}{a} \quad \Rightarrow \quad 1 = \frac{\sqrt{p^2 - 4\cdot 1\cdot q}}{1} \Rightarrow p^2 - 4q = 1$$

Since p is positive, $p = \sqrt{4q+1}$.

Example 13. When $a < m \le b$, the equation $(m+3)x^2 - mx + 1 = 0$ has two negative solutions. Find the value ab.

Solution: 6.

Let x_1 and x_2 be the two roots.

We know that $\Delta \geq 0$ when the quadratic equation has two real solutions

$$(-m)^2 - 4(m+3) \geq 0 \quad \Rightarrow \quad m^2 - 4m - 12 \geq 0 \tag{1}$$

By Vieta's Theorem, $x_1 + x_2 = -(-\dfrac{m}{m+3}) = \dfrac{m}{m+3}$

and $x_1 x_2 = \dfrac{1}{m+3}$.

Since both x_1 and x_2 are negative, $\dfrac{m}{m+3} < 0$ \hfill (2)

and $\dfrac{1}{m+3} > 0$ \hfill (3)

From (1), we have $m \geq 6$ and $m \leq -2$.

From (3), we have $m > -3$.

From (2), we have $-3 < m < 0$.

So the solution will be $-3 < m \leq -2$.

The answer is then $ab = (-3) \times (-2) = 6$.

Example 14. Two roots of the equation $2x^2 - 8nx + 10x - n^2 + 35n - 76 = 0$ are prime numbers. What is the greatest possible value of x?

Solution: 5.

Let x_1 and x_2 be the two roots.

By Vieta's Theorem, $x_1 + x_2 = -\dfrac{10 - 8n}{2} = 4n - 5$

Since both x_1 and x_2 are prime numbers, and $4n - 5$ is odd, one of them must be 2. So the original equation can be written as $2 \times 2^2 - 8n \times 2 - 10 \times 2 - n^2 + 35n - 76 = 0$, or $n^2 - 19n + 48 = 0 \quad \Rightarrow \quad (n - 16)(n - 3) = 0$.
Solving we get: $n = 16$ or 3.

When $n = 16$, the original equation can be written as

$2x^2 - 8 \times 16x + 10x - 16^2 + 35 \times 16 - 76 = 0$ or $x^2 - 59x + 114 = 0$.
Solving we have $x = 2$ and 57 (not a prime number).

When $n = 3$, the original equation can be written as
$2x^2 - 8 \times 3x + 10x - 3^2 + 35 \times 3 - 76 = 0$ or $x^2 - 7x + 10 = 0$.
Solving we have $x = 2$ and 5.
The greatest possible value of x is 5.

Example 15. How many values of k are there such that the quadratic equation $kx^2 + (k+1)x + (k-1) = 0$ has integer solutions?

Solution: 2.
Since this is a quadratic equation, $k \neq 0$.
Let x_1 and x_2 be the two integer solutions.

By Vieta's Theorem, $x_1 + x_2 = -\dfrac{k+1}{k} = -1 - \dfrac{1}{k}$ (1)

and $x_1 x_2 = \dfrac{k-1}{k} = 1 - \dfrac{1}{k}$ (2)

(2) − (1): $x_1 + x_2 - x_1 x_2 = 2$ $\Rightarrow$ $(x_1 - 1)(x_2 - 1) = 3$.
We know that x_1 and x_2 be the two integers. So we have

$$\begin{cases} x_1 - 1 = 3 \\ x_2 - 1 = 1 \end{cases} \qquad \begin{cases} x_1 - 1 = 1 \\ x_2 - 1 = 3 \end{cases}$$

or

$$\begin{cases} x_1 - 1 = -3 \\ x_2 - 1 = -1 \end{cases} \qquad \begin{cases} x_1 - 1 = -1 \\ x_2 - 1 = -3 \end{cases}$$

Solving we have $x_1 + x_2 = 6$ or $x_1 + x_2 = -2$.

Thus $-1 - \dfrac{1}{k} = 6$ $\Rightarrow$ $-\dfrac{1}{k} = 7$ $\Rightarrow$ $k = -\dfrac{1}{7}$

or $-1 - \dfrac{1}{k} = -2$ $\Rightarrow$ $-\dfrac{1}{k} = -1$ $\Rightarrow$ $k = 1$.

We checked and both values work.

Example 16. Two of the roots of the equation $2x^3 + 3x^2 - 23x - 12 = 0$ are 3 and -4. What is the third root? Express your answer as a common fraction.

Solution: $-\dfrac{1}{2}$.

By Vieta's Theorem, the sum of the three roots is equal to

$$x_1 + x_2 + x_3 = -\frac{3}{2}.$$

We are given that two of the roots are 3 and -4, so substituting in these values,

we get $3 - 4 + x_3 = \dfrac{3}{2} \implies \quad x_3 = -\dfrac{1}{2}$.

Example 17. A cubic equation of the form $x^3 + bx^2 + cx + d = 0$ has solutions $x = 3$, $x = 4$ and $x = 5$. What are the values of b, c and d? Express your answer as an ordered triple (b, c, d).

Solution: $(-12, 47, -60)$.

$$x_1 + x_2 + x_3 = -b \tag{1}$$

$$x_1 x_2 + x_2 x_3 + x_3 x_1 = c \tag{2}$$

$$x_1 x_2 x_3 = -d \tag{3}$$

$3 + 4 + 5 = -b \qquad\qquad \implies \qquad b = -12.$

$3 \times 4 + 4 \times 5 + 5 \times 3 = c \qquad \implies \qquad c = 47$

$3 \times 4 \times 5 = -d \qquad\qquad \implies \qquad d = -60.$

Example 18. What is the sum of the reciprocals of the solutions of $x^3 - 3x^2 - 13x + 15 = 0$? Express your answer as a common fraction.

Solution: $\dfrac{13}{15}$.

$$\frac{1}{r}+\frac{1}{s}+\frac{1}{t}=\frac{st+rt+rs}{rst}=\frac{-13}{-15}=\frac{13}{15}.$$

Example 19. What is the sum of the squares of the solutions of $x^3-2x^2-3x-1=0$?

Solution: 10.

If r, s, t are roots, by Vieta's Theorem,

$r+s+t=2$

$rs+st+tr=-3$

$rst=1$.

$r^2+s^2+t^2=(r+s+t)^2-2(rs+st+tr)=(2)^2-2\times(-3)=10$.

Example 20. If r, s, t are roots of the solutions of $x^3-2x^2-3x-1=0$, determine the value of $\dfrac{1}{r^2}+\dfrac{1}{s^2}+\dfrac{1}{t^2}$.

Solution: 5.

If r, s, t are roots, by Vieta's Theorem,

$r+s+t=2$ (1)

$rs+st+tr=-3$ (2)

$rst=1$.   (3)

We know that

$r^2+s^2+t^2=(r+s+t)^2-2(rs+st+tr)=(2)^2-2\times(-3)=10$.

Squaring both sides of (2): $(rs+st+tr)^2=(-3)^2\Rightarrow$

$(rs)^2+(st)^2+(tr)^2+2(rsst+sttr+trrs)=9\Rightarrow$

$(rs)^2+(st)^2+(tr)^2+2(s+t+r)=9\Rightarrow(rs)^2+(st)^2+(tr)^2+2(2)=9\Rightarrow$

$(rs)^2+(st)^2+(tr)^2)=9-4=5$ (4)

Therefore $\dfrac{1}{r^2}+\dfrac{1}{s^2}+\dfrac{1}{t^2}=\dfrac{(st)^2+(rt)^2+(rs)^2}{(rst)^2}=\dfrac{5}{(1)^2}=5$.

Example 21. (2014 Mathcounts State Sprint Problem 27) The fourth degree polynomial equation $x^4-7x^3+4x^2+7x-4=0$ has four real roots, a, b, c and d. What is the value of the sum $\dfrac{1}{a}+\dfrac{1}{b}+\dfrac{1}{c}+\dfrac{1}{d}$? Express your answer as a common fraction.

Solution: $\dfrac{7}{4}$.

By the Vieta's Theorem, $abcd=\dfrac{-4}{1}=-4$ and $bcd+acd+abd+abc=-\dfrac{7}{1}=-7$.

Thus $\dfrac{1}{a}+\dfrac{1}{b}+\dfrac{1}{c}+\dfrac{1}{d}=\dfrac{bcd+acd+abc}{abcd}=\dfrac{-7}{-4}=\dfrac{7}{4}$.

3. APPLICATIONS OF THE CONVERSE OF VIETA'S THEOREM

If a problem contains the sum and the product of two numbers, the converse of Vieta's Theorem can be used to construct a quadratic equation directly.

Example 22. How many distinct ordered triples (x, y, z) satisfy the equations
$$\begin{cases} x+y+z=9 \\ xy+yz+zx=26 \\ xyz=24 \end{cases}$$

Solution: 6.

x, y, and z are the solutions to the following equation: $t^3-9t^2+26t-24=0 \Rightarrow$

Or $(t-2)(t-4)(t-3)=0$

So the solutions are (2, 3, 4). This can be permutated in 6 different ways, as shown below.

$$\begin{cases} x = 4 \\ y = 2 \\ z = 3 \end{cases} \qquad \begin{cases} x = 4 \\ y = 3 \\ z = 2 \end{cases} \qquad \begin{cases} x = 2 \\ y = 3 \\ z = 4 \end{cases}$$

$$\begin{cases} x = 2 \\ y = 4 \\ z = 3 \end{cases} \qquad \begin{cases} x = 3 \\ y = 2 \\ z = 4 \end{cases} \qquad \begin{cases} x = 3 \\ y = 4 \\ z = 2 \end{cases}$$

Thus, the original system has 6 distinct solutions.

Example 23. Find the value of $x^{2015} + y^{2015} - z^{2015}$ for real x, y, and z satisfying the following system of equations:

$$\begin{cases} x + y = 2 \\ xy - z^2 = 1 \end{cases}$$

Solution: 2.

Since $x + y = 2$ and $xy = 1 + z^2$, we know that x and y are two real roots of

$$t^2 - 2t + 1 + z^2 = 0 \qquad\qquad (1)$$

The discriminant of this quadratic must be greater than or equal to 0 in order for the quadratic to attain real number solutions, so

$$\Delta = 4 - 4(1 + z^2) \geq 0 \qquad\Rightarrow\qquad z^2 \leq 0$$

But we know that $z^2 \geq 0$, so $z = 0$.

Substituting $z = 0$ into (1), we have $t^2 - 2t + 1 = 0$.

Solve for t: $t_1 = t_2 = 1$. Therefore, $x = y = 1$.

The solutions:

$$\begin{cases} x = y = 1 \\ z = 0 \end{cases}$$

The answer is $x^{2015} + y^{2015} - z^{2015} = 1 + 1 - 0 = 2$.

If the problem contains the sum of two numbers, we can find the product of these two numbers, and then construct the quadratic equation.

Similarly, if the problem contains the product of two numbers, we can find the sum of these two numbers, and then construct the quadratic equation. See the example below.

Example 24. Find the greatest real value of z such that $x + y + z = 5$ and $xy + yz + zx = 3$. x and y are real numbers. Express your answer as a common fraction.

Solution: $\dfrac{13}{3}$.

$$x + y = 5 - z \tag{1}$$
$$xy = 3 - z(x + y) = 3 - z(5 - z) = z^2 - 5z + 3 \tag{2}$$

From (1) and (2), we know that x and y are two real roots of the quadratic $t^2 - (5 - z)t + z^2 - 5z + 3 = 0$.

The discriminant of this quadratic must be greater than or equal to 0 in order for the quadratic to attain real number solutions.

Therefore $\Delta = (5 - z)^2 - 4(z^2 - 5z + 3) \geq 0$.

$3z^2 - 10z - 13 \leq 0$.

Solve for z: $-1 \leq z \leq \dfrac{13}{3}$.

The greatest value of z is $\dfrac{13}{3}$.

Example 25. Find the greatest possible value of $x_1^2 + x_2^2$ if x_1 and x_2 are two real roots of $x^2 - (k - 2)x + (k^2 + 3k + 5) = 0$. k is real.

154

Solution: 18.

By Vieta's Theorem:
$$x_1^2 + x_2^2 = (x_1 + x_2)^2 - 2x_1x_2 = (k-2)^2 - 2(k^2 + 3k + 5)$$
$$= -(k+5)^2 + 19$$

Since the equation has two real roots, the discriminant of the quadratic equation must be greater than or equal to 0, so
$$\Delta = (k-2)^2 - 4(k^2 + 3k + 5) \geq 0$$
Or $3k^2 + 16k + 16 \leq 0$.

Solving this inequality gives: $-4 \leq k \leq -\dfrac{4}{3}$.

In this range, the greatest value of $x_1^2 + x_2^2$ can be achieved by letting $k = -4$.
So the greatest possible value of $x_1^2 + x_2^2 = 18$ (not 19!).

Example 26. (1976 AMC Problem 30) How many distinct ordered triples (x, y, z) satisfy the equations
$$x + 2y + 4z = 12$$
$$xy + 4yz + 2xz = 22$$
$$xyz = 6?$$
(A) none   (B) 1   (C) 2   (D) 4   (E) 6

Solution: (E).
Method 1 (official solution):
We observe that we can find a system of symmetric equations by the following change of variables:
$$x = 2u, \qquad y = v, \qquad z = \frac{1}{2}w \qquad\qquad (1)$$

This substitution yields the transformed system
$$u + v + w = 6,$$
$$uv + vw + uw = 11, \qquad\qquad (2)$$
$$uvw = 6.$$

Consider the polynomial $p(t) = (t - u)(t - v)(t - w)$, where (u, v, w) is a solution of equation (2).

Then $p(t) = t^3 - 6t^2 + 11t - 6,$ (3)

And u, v, w are the solutions of $p(t) = 0$.

Conversely, if the roots of $p(t) = 0$ are listed as a triple in any order, this triple is a solution to equation (2).

It is not hard to see that $p(t) = 0$ has three distinct solutions. In fact,
$p(t) = (t - 1)(t - 2)(t - 3)$.

So the triple $(1, 2, 3)$ and each of its permutations satisfies the equation (2).

Since the change of variables (1) is one-to-one, the original system has 6 distinct

solutions (x, y, z): $(2, 3, 1)$, $(2, 2, \frac{3}{2})$, $(4, 1, \frac{3}{2})$, $(4, 3, \frac{1}{2})$, $(6, 1, 1)$ or $(6, 2, \frac{1}{2})$.

Method 2 (our solution):

Let $a = x$, $b = 2y$, and $c = 4z$.

The system of equations becomes:

$a + b + c = 12$

$ab + bc + ac = 44$

$abc = 48$

a, b, and c are the solutions to the following equation: $t^3 - 12t^2 + 44t - 48 = 0$

We observe that 2 is a solution of the cubic above.

By long division, we can factor the cubic into: $(t - 2)(t^2 - 10t + 24) = 0$

Or $(t - 2)(t - 4)(t - 6) = 0$

So the solutions are $(2, 4, 6)$. This can be permutated in 6 different ways, as shown below.

$$\begin{cases} a = 2 \\ b = 4 \\ c = 6 \end{cases} \implies \begin{cases} x = 2 \\ y = \dfrac{b}{2} = 2 \\ z = \dfrac{c}{4} = \dfrac{3}{2} \end{cases} \qquad \begin{cases} a = 2 \\ b = 6 \\ c = 4 \end{cases} \implies \begin{cases} x = 2 \\ y = \dfrac{b}{2} = 3 \\ z = \dfrac{c}{4} = 1 \end{cases}$$

$$\begin{cases} a = 4 \\ b = 2 \\ c = 6 \end{cases} \implies \begin{cases} x = 4 \\ y = \dfrac{b}{2} = 1 \\ z = \dfrac{c}{4} = \dfrac{3}{2} \end{cases} \qquad \begin{cases} a = 4 \\ b = 6 \\ c = 2 \end{cases} \implies \begin{cases} x = 4 \\ y = \dfrac{b}{2} = 3 \\ z = \dfrac{c}{4} = \dfrac{1}{2} \end{cases}$$

$$\begin{cases} a = 6 \\ b = 2 \\ c = 4 \end{cases} \implies \begin{cases} x = 6 \\ y = \dfrac{b}{2} = 1 \\ z = \dfrac{c}{4} = 1 \end{cases} \qquad \begin{cases} a = 6 \\ b = 4 \\ c = 2 \end{cases} \implies \begin{cases} x = 6 \\ y = \dfrac{b}{2} = 2 \\ z = \dfrac{c}{4} = \dfrac{1}{2} \end{cases}$$

Thus, the original system has 6 distinct solutions.

PROBLEMS

Problem 1. Find k if the sum of the reciprocals of two roots of the equation $4x^2 - 8x + k = 0$ is $\dfrac{8}{3}$.

Problem 2. Find $\alpha^3 + \beta^3$ if α and β are two roots of the equation $2x^2 + 5x - 3 = 0$. Express your answer as a mixed number.

Problem 3. (1955 AMC) Two numbers whose sum is 6 and the absolute value of whose difference is 8 are roots of the equation:
(A) $x^2 - 6x + 7 = 0$ (B) $x^2 - 6x - 7 = 0$ (C) $x^2 + 6x - 8 = 0$
(D) $x^2 - 6x + 8 = 0$ (E) $x^2 + 6x - 7 = 0$

Problem 4. A quadratic equation of the form $x^2 + kx + m = 0$ has solutions $x = 3 + 2\sqrt{2}$ and $x = 3 - 2\sqrt{2}$. What is the value of $k + m$?

Problem 5. If r and s are the solutions of $2x^2 + 9x + 3 = 0$, what is the value of $r^2 + s^2$? Express your answer as a common fraction.

Problem 6. The solutions of $x^2 + bx + c = 0$ are each 5 more than the solutions of $x^2 + 7x + 3 = 0$. What are the values of b and c? Express your answer as an ordered pair (b, c).

Problem 7. m and n are two roots of the quadratic equation $x^2 + 2016x + 7 = 0$. Determine the value of $(m^2 + 2015m + 6)(n^2 + 2017n + 8)$.

Problem 8. The difference of two real roots of the equation $x^2 + px + 1 = 0$ $(p > 0)$ is 1. What is the value for p? Express your answer in simplest radical form.

Problem 9. Find the value of $\dfrac{b}{a} + \dfrac{a}{b}$ if $a^2 + 3a + 1 = 0$ and $b^2 + 3b + 1 = 0$. $a \neq b$.

Problem 10. (2011 Mathcounts Handbook Problem 248) Three numbers have a sum of 5 and the sum of their squares is 29. If the product of the three numbers is -10, what is the least of the three numbers? Express your answer in simplest radical form.

Problem 11. (2014 Mathcounts State Sprint Round) The nonzero roots of the equation $x^2 + 6x + k = 0$ are in the ratio 2:1. What is the value of k?

Problem 12. Find the smallest positive value of $x + y$ if $x + y = x \cdot y$.

Problem 13. Solve $\sqrt{\dfrac{a-x}{b+x}} + \sqrt{\dfrac{b+x}{a-x}} = 2$ if $a > b > 0$.

Problem 14. $\sqrt{28 - 10\sqrt{3}}$ is a root of the quadratic equation $x^2 + ax + b = 0$. Both a and b are rational numbers. Determine the value of ab.

Problem 15. Find $\dfrac{1}{\alpha^3} + \dfrac{1}{\beta^3}$ if α and β are two roots of the equation

$x^2 - x - 3 = 0$ Express your answer as a common fraction.

Problem 16. The positive difference of two real roots of the equation $x^2 - 4ax + 5a^2 - 6a = 0$ is 6. What is the value for a?

Problem 17. a^2 and b^2 are two roots of the quadratic equation $x^2 - cx + c = 0$. Determine the value of $a\sqrt{1 - \dfrac{1}{b^2}} + b\sqrt{1 - \dfrac{1}{a^2}}$. Both a and b are positive real numbers.

Problem 18. Find the smallest possible value of $x_1^2 + x_2^2$ if x_1 and x_2 are two real roots of $x^2 - kx + 2k - 3 = 0$. k is real.

Problem 19. The quadratic equation $2x^2 + x - 1 = 0$ has two roots, a and b. What is the value of $\dfrac{1}{a^3b^2} - \dfrac{2}{a^2b} - \dfrac{2}{ab^2} + \dfrac{1}{a^2b^3}$?

Problem 20. Two roots of the equation $\dfrac{1}{2}px^2 - \dfrac{1}{2}qx + 2017 = 0$ are prime numbers. p and q are positive integers. What is the value of $2p + q$?

Problem 21. The quadratic equation $(k-1)x^2 - px + k = 0$ has two positive integer solutions. k is a positive integer. What is the value of $13 \times 31 \times (k + p)$?

Problem 22. If the sum of the squares of two real roots of the equation $x^2 - (k+1)x + k + 2 = 0$ is 6, find the value of k.

Problem 23. The quadratic equation $x^2 - 2ax + 4a - 3 = 0$ has two positive integer solutions each greater than 1. What is the smallest positive integer value of a?

Problem 24. What is the sum of the squares of the solutions of $x^3 - 15x^2 + 66x - 80 = 0$?

Problem 25. The solutions of $x^3 - 63x^2 + cx - 1728 = 0$ form a geometric sequence. What is the value of c?

Problem 26. (2004 North Carolina State Mathematics Contest) Two of the roots of the equation $2x^3 - 3x^2 + px + q = 0$ are 3 and -2. What is the third root? Express your answer as a common fraction.

Problem 27. (1975 AMC #27) If p, q and r are distinct roots of $x^3 - x^2 + x - 2 = 0$, then $p^3 + q^3 + r^3$ equals
(A) -1 (B) 1   (C)3   (D) 5   (E) none of these

Problem 28. (1996 AIME) Suppose that the roots of $x^3 + 3x^2 + 4x - 11 = 0$ are a, b, and c, and that the roots of $x^3 + rx^2 + sx + t = 0$ are $a + b$, $b + c$, and $c + a$. Find t.

Problem 29. (1984 USAMO) The product of two of the four roots of the quartic equation $x^4 - 18x^3 + kx^2 + 200x - 1984 = 0$ is -32. Determine the value of k.

SOLUTIONS TO PROBLEMS

Problem 1. Solution: 3.

Let the two roots be x_1 and x_2.

$$\frac{1}{x_1} + \frac{1}{x_2} = \frac{8}{3}.$$

By Vieta's Theorem, $x_1 x_2 = \frac{k}{4}$ and $x_1 + x_2 = 2$.

Since $\dfrac{1}{x_1} + \dfrac{1}{x_2} = \dfrac{x_1 + x_2}{x_1 x_2}$, $\dfrac{2}{\frac{k}{4}} = \dfrac{8}{3}$. $\therefore$ $k = 3$.

Problem 2. Solution: $-26\dfrac{7}{8}$.

By Vieta's Theorem,

$$\alpha + \beta = -\frac{5}{2}, \qquad \alpha \cdot \beta = -\frac{3}{2}.$$

$$\alpha^3 + \beta^3 = -\frac{b(\alpha^2 + \beta^2) + c(\alpha + \beta)}{\alpha}$$

$$\alpha^3 + \beta^3 = -\frac{5 \cdot \dfrac{37}{4} + (-3)(-\dfrac{5}{2})}{2} = -\frac{215}{8} = -26\frac{7}{8}.$$

Problem 3. Solution: B.

Let α and β be the two numbers.

By Vieta's Theorem:

$\alpha + \beta = 6$ (1)

$|\alpha - \beta| = 8$ (2)

$(1)^2 - (2)^2$: $4\alpha\beta = -28$ $\Rightarrow$ $\alpha\beta = -7$

Therefore α and β be the two roots of the quadratic $x^2 - 6x - 7 = 0$.

Problem 4. Solution: -5.

By Vieta's Theorem, $-k$ is the sum of the solutions and m is the product of the solutions.

So $-k = 3 + 2\sqrt{2} + 3 - 2\sqrt{2} = 6 \implies k = -6.$

$m = (3 + 2\sqrt{2})(3 - 2\sqrt{2}) = 1.$

Therefore, the value of $k + m = -6 + 1 = -5.$

Problem 5. Solution: $\dfrac{69}{4}$.

Applying the Vieta's Theorem:

$$r^2 + s^2 = (r+s)^2 - 2rs = (-\frac{9}{2})^2 - 2 \times \frac{3}{2} = \frac{81}{4} - 3 = \frac{69}{4}.$$

Problem 6. Solution: $(-3, -7)$.

$r + s + 10 = -b \qquad \implies \qquad -7 + 10 = -b \implies \qquad b = -3.$

$(r + 5)(s + 5) = c \qquad \implies \qquad rs + 5(r + s) + 25 = c \implies \qquad 3 + 5(-7) + 25 = c$

$\implies \qquad c = -7.$

Problem 7. Solution: 2008.

By Vieta's Theorem, $mn = -\dfrac{2016}{1} = -2016$, and $m + n = \dfrac{7}{1} = 7$.

$m^2 + 2015m + 6 = m^2 + 2016m + 7 - (m+1) = -(m+1)$

$n^2 + 2017n + 8 = n^2 + 2016n + 8 + (n+1) = (n+1)$

$(m^2 + 2015m + 6)(n^2 + 2017n + 8) = -(m+1)(n+1) = -mn - (m+n) - 1$

$= -(-2016) - 7 - 1 = 2016 - 8 = 2008.$

Problem 8. Solution: $\sqrt{5}$.

We know that the equation has two real roots. So we have $\Delta = p^2 - 4 > 0 \implies$

$\qquad p^2 > 4 \implies \qquad p > 2.$

Let x_1 and x_2 be the two roots.

By Vieta's Theorem, $x_1 + x_2 = -p$ and $x_1 \times x_2 = 1$.

$(x_1 - x_2)^2 = (x_1 + x_2)^2 - 4x_1 x_2 = 1$.

So $1^2 = (-p)^2 - 4$ $\Rightarrow$ $p^2 = 5 \Rightarrow$ $p = \sqrt{5}$.

Problem 9. Solution: 7.

We know that $a^2 + 3a + 1 = 0$ and $b^2 + 3b + 1 = 0$. We also know that $a \neq b$. So a and b are two distinct real roots of the equation $x^2 + 3x + 1 = 0$ ($\Delta = (3)^2 - 4\,(1) = 5 > 0$).

Thus $a + b = -3$
          $ab = 1$

$$\frac{b}{a} + \frac{a}{b} = \frac{b^2 + a^2}{ab} = a^2 + b^2 = (a+b)^2 - 2ab = (-3)^2 - 2 = 7$$

Problem 10. Solution: $-\sqrt{2}$.

$a + b + c = 5$	(1)
$a^2 + b^2 + c^2 = 29$	(2)
$abc = -10$	(3)

Squaring both sides of (1): $(a+b+c)^2 = 25 \Rightarrow a^2 + b^2 + c^2 + 2(ab + bc + ca) = 25$

$ab + bc + ca = -2$	(4)

$a + b + c = 5$	(1)
$ab + bc + ca = -2$	(4)
$abc = -10$	(3)

By Vieta's Theorem, $a + b + c =$ are the three roots of the equation:

$x^3 - 5x^2 - 2x + 10 = 0 \Rightarrow x^2(x-5) - 2(x-5) = 0$ $\Rightarrow$ $(x-5)(x^2-2) = 0$.

The three roots are 5, $\sqrt{2}$, and $-\sqrt{2}$.

The least of them is $-\sqrt{2}$.

Problem 11. Solution: 8.

Let x_1 and x_2 be the two roots.

$x_1 = 2x_2$ (1)

By Vieta's Theorem, $x_1 + x_2 = -6$ (2)

Substituting (1) into (2): $2x_2 + x_2 = -6 \Rightarrow \quad 3x_2 = -6 \quad\quad \Rightarrow \quad\quad x_2 = -2$.

Substituting the value of x_2 into the original equation: $(-2)^2 + 6(-2) + k = 0 \Rightarrow$

$k = 8$.

Problem 12. Solution: 4.

Let $x + y = x \cdot y = k > 0$. x and y are two real roots of $t^2 - kt + k = 0$.

Therefore $\Delta = (-k)^2 - 4k \geq 0$.

$k \geq 4$ so the smallest positive value of $x + y$, or $(x+y)_{min}$, equals 4.

Problem 13. Solution: $x = \dfrac{1}{2}(a-b)$

Notice that $\sqrt{\dfrac{a-x}{b+x}} \cdot \sqrt{\dfrac{b+x}{a-x}} = 1$.

By Vieta's Theorem, $\sqrt{\dfrac{a-x}{b+x}}$ and $\sqrt{\dfrac{b+x}{a-x}}$ are two roots of the quadratic equation

$t^2 - 2t + 1 = 0 \quad\quad\quad \Rightarrow \quad\quad t_1 = t_2 = 1$.

Therefore $\sqrt{\dfrac{a-x}{b+x}} = 1 \quad\quad\quad \Rightarrow \quad\quad x = \dfrac{1}{2}(a-b)$.

To double check, we can substitute $x = \dfrac{1}{2}(a-b)$ into the original equation, and see

that it is indeed the root of the original equation.

Problem 14. Solution: -220.

$\sqrt{28 - 10\sqrt{3}} = \sqrt{5^2 - 2\times 5\sqrt{3} + (\sqrt{3})^2} = \sqrt{(5-\sqrt{3})^2} = 5 - \sqrt{3}$.

Since the coefficients of the equation are all rational numbers, the other root of the equation is $5+\sqrt{3}$.

By Vieta's Theorem, $x_1 + x_2 = a = -[(5-\sqrt{3})+(5+\sqrt{3})] = -10.$

and $x_1 x_2 = b = (5-\sqrt{3})(5+\sqrt{3}) = 25 - 3 = 22.$

Thus $ab = 22 \times (-10) = -220.$

Problem 15. Solution: $-\dfrac{10}{27}$.

$$\frac{1}{\alpha^3} + \frac{1}{\beta^3} = -\frac{10}{27}.$$

Problem 16. Solution: 3.

Let x_1 and x_2 be the two roots.

By Vieta's Theorem, $x_1 + x_2 = 4a$ and $x_1 x_2 = 5a^2 - 6a$.

We are given that $|x_1 - x_2| = 6$ \hfill (1)

Squaring both sides of the equation (1): $(x_1 - x_2)^2 = (x_1 + x_2)^2 - 4x_1 x_2 = 36$.

$\Rightarrow$ So $(4a)^2 - 4(5a^2 - 6a) = 36$ $\Rightarrow$ $16a^2 - 20a^2 + 24a = 36$

$\Rightarrow$ $4a^2 - 24a + 36 = 0$ $\Rightarrow a^2 - 6a + 9 = 0 \Rightarrow (a-3)^2 = 0$ $\Rightarrow$ $a = 3$.

Problem 17. Solution: 2.

By Vieta's Theorem, $a^2 + b^2 = c$ and $a^2 b^2 = c$.

So $a^2 + b^2 = a^2 b^2$ \hfill (1)

We divide both sides of equation (1) by a^2: $1 + \dfrac{b^2}{a^2} = b^2$ $\Rightarrow \dfrac{b^2}{a^2} = b^2 - 1$ (2)

We divide both sides of equation (1) by b^2: $\dfrac{a^2}{b^2} + 1 = a^2$ $\Rightarrow \dfrac{a^2}{b^2} = a^2 - 1$ (3)

$a\sqrt{1 - \dfrac{1}{b^2}} + b\sqrt{1 - \dfrac{1}{a^2}}$ can be rewritten as $\sqrt{a^2 - \dfrac{a^2}{b^2}} + \sqrt{b^2 - \dfrac{b^2}{a^2}}$.

Considering (2) and (3) we get

$$a\sqrt{1-\frac{1}{b^2}}+b\sqrt{1-\frac{1}{a^2}}=\sqrt{a^2-(a^2-1)}+\sqrt{b^2-(b^2-1)}=1+1=2.$$

Problem 18. Solution: 2.

Since the equation has two real roots, $\Delta \geq 0$. That is

$$k^2-4(2k-3)\geq 0 \qquad \Rightarrow \qquad k^2-8k+12\geq 0 \tag{1}$$

Solving the inequality (1): $k\leq 2$ or $k\geq 6$.

By Vieta's Theorem, $x_1+x_2=-(-k)=k$ (2)

and $x_1 x_2 = 2k-3$ (3)

Squaring both sides of the equation (2): $(x_1+x_2)^2=x_1^2+x_2^2+2x_1 x_2=k^2$ (4)

Substituting (3) into (4): $x_1^2+x_2^2+2(2k-3)=k^2$

$\Rightarrow \qquad x_1^2+x_2^2=k^2-4k+6=k^2-2k\times 2+2^2+2=(k-2)^2+2$.

The smallest value of $x_1^2+x_2^2$ is 2 when $k=2$.

Problem 19. Solution: 8.

By Vieta's Theorem, $a+b=-\dfrac{1}{2}$ (1)

and $ab=\dfrac{-1}{2}=-\dfrac{1}{2}$ (2)

$$\frac{1}{a^3 b^2}-\frac{2}{a^2 b}-\frac{2}{ab^2}+\frac{1}{a^2 b^3}=\frac{1}{a^3 b^2}+\frac{1}{a^2 b^3}-\frac{2}{a^2 b}-\frac{2}{ab^2}$$

$$=\frac{1}{a^2 b^2}(\frac{1}{a}+\frac{1}{b})-\frac{2}{ab}(\frac{1}{a}+\frac{1}{b})=\frac{1}{a^2 b^2}(\frac{a+b}{ab})-\frac{2}{ab}(\frac{a+b}{ab})$$

$$=\frac{a+b}{(ab)^2}(\frac{1}{ab}-2)=\frac{-\dfrac{1}{2}}{(-\dfrac{1}{2})^2}(\frac{1}{-\dfrac{1}{2}}-2)=(-2)\times(-4)=8$$

167

Problem 20. Solution: 2021.

The original equation can be written as $px^2 - qx + 2017 \times 2 = 0$

Let x_1 and x_2 be the two roots.

By Vieta's Theorem, $x_1 x_2 = -\dfrac{2017 \times 2}{p}$

Since both x_1 and x_2 are prime numbers, and p is an integer, $p = 1$ and one of the two roots must be 2 and the other must be 2017.

By Vieta's Theorem, $x_1 + x_2 = -\dfrac{-q}{p} = q \quad \Rightarrow \quad 2 + 2017 = q = 2019$.

The answer is $2p + q = 2 \times 1 + 2019 = 2021$.

Problem 21. Solution: 2015.

Since this is a quadratic equation, $k - 1 \neq 0$. So $k \geq 2$.

Let x_1 and x_2 be the two roots.

By Vieta's Theorem, $x_1 + x_2 = -\dfrac{-p}{k-1} = \dfrac{p}{k-1}$ (1)

and $x_1 x_2 = \dfrac{k}{k-1} = 1 + \dfrac{1}{k-1}$ (2)

Since both x_1 and x_2 are positive integers, the product $x_1 x_2$ must be an integer.

From (2) we see that $\dfrac{1}{k-1}$ must be an integer. So $k - 1 = 1$ or $k = 2$.

Thus one of x_1 and x_2 must be 1 and the other must be 3. So $x_1 + x_2 = 3$.

(1) becomes: $3 = \dfrac{p}{1} \quad \Rightarrow \quad p = 3$.

The answer is $13 \times 31 \times (k + p) = 13 \times 31 \times (2 + 3) = = 13 \times 31 \times 5 = 2015$.

Problem 22. Solution: -3.

Let the two roots be r and s.

By Vieta's Theorem, $r + s = k + 1$, and $rs = k + 2$.

So $r^2 + s^2 = (r + s)^2 - 2rs = (k + 1)^2 - 2 \times (k + 2) = k^2 - 3$.

$k^2 - 3 = 6 \quad \Rightarrow \quad k^2 = 9$.

We get $k = -3$ or $k = 3$.

When $k = 3$, $\Delta = (3+1)^2 - 4(3+2) < 0$. The equation has no real solutions.

When $k = -3$, $\Delta = (-3+1)^2 - 4(-3+2) > 0$. So the answer is -3.

Problem 23. Solution: 3.

Let $x = y + 1$. The original equation can be written as

$y^2 - 2(a-1)y + 2(a-1) = 0$.

We know that the quadratic equation $x^2 - 2ax + 4a - 3 = 0$ has two positive integer solutions. Therefore

$$\Delta = 4(a-1)^2 - 8(a-1) \geq 0 \quad \Rightarrow \quad 4a^2 - 16a + 12) \geq 0 \quad \Rightarrow a^2 - 4a + 3) \geq 0$$
$$\Rightarrow (a-3)(a-1) \geq 0 \qquad\qquad (1)$$

By Vieta's Theorem, $y_1 + y_2 = 2(a-1) > 0$ \hfill (2)

and $y_1 y_2 = 2(a-1) > 0$ \hfill (3)

Solving the system of inequalities (1), (2), and (3): $a \geq 3$.

The smallest integer value for a is 3.

Problem 24. Solution: 93.

$r^2 + s^2 + t^2 = (r+s+t)^2 - 2(rs+st+tr) = [-(-15)]^2 - 2 \times 66 = 93$.

Problem 25. Solution: 756.

$r + s + t = -(-63)$ \hfill (1)

$rs + st + tr = c$ \hfill (2)

$rst = -(-1728)$ \hfill (3)

We know that $s^2 = rt$ \hfill (4)

Substituting (4) into (3): $s^3 = 1728 \quad \Rightarrow \quad s = 12$.

$12(r+t) + s^2 = c \quad \Rightarrow \quad 12(r+t) + 144 = c$ \hfill (5)

Substituting (1) into (5): $c = 612 + 144 = 756$.

Problem 26. Solution: $\dfrac{1}{2}$.

By Vieta's Theorem, the sum of the three roots is equal to

$$x_1 + x_2 + x_3 = -\dfrac{3}{2}.$$

We are given that two of the roots are 3 and -2, so substituting in these values,

we get $3 - 2 - x_3 = -\dfrac{3}{2}$ $\Rightarrow$ $x_3 = \dfrac{1}{2}$.

Problem 27. Solution: (E).
(Official Solution):
 If p, q, r are roots, then the polynomial can be factored as follows:
$$x^3 - x^2 + x - 2 = (x - p)(x - q)(x - r)$$
$$= x^3 - (p + q + r)x^2 + (pq + pr + qr)x - pqr.$$
Equating coefficients of like powers of x, we find
$$p + q + r = 1, \quad pq + pr + qr = 1, \quad pqr = 2.$$
In looking for the sum of the cubes of the roots of a cubic equation, let us use the fact that each root satisfies the equation:
$$p^3 - p^2 + p - 2 = 0$$
$$q^3 - q^2 + q - 2 = 0$$
$$r^3 - r^2 + r - 2 = 0.$$
Adding these, we obtain
$$(*)\ p^3 + q^3 + r^3 - (p^2 + q^2 + r^2) + (p + q + r) - 6 = 0.$$
We saw that $p + q + r = 1$ and shall determine the sum of the squares of the roots by squaring this relation:
$$(p + q + r)^2 = p^2 + q^2 + r^2 + 2(pq + pr + qr) = 1$$
$$p^2 + q^2 + r^2 + 2(1) = 1$$
$$p^2 + q^2 + r^2 = -1.$$
Substituting this into (*), we obtain $p^3 + q^3 + r^3 = -1 - 1 + 6 = 4$.

Problem 28. Solution: 23.

Applying Vieta's Theorem to the $x^3 + 3x^2 + 4x - 11 = 0$:

$a + b + c = -3$

$ab + bc + ca = 4$

$abc = 11$

So $a + b = -3 - c$, $b + c = -3 - a$, and $c + a = -3 - b$.

Applying Vieta's Theorem to $x^3 + rx^2 + st + t = 0$:

$t = -(a + b)(b + c)(c + a) = -(-3 - c)(-3 - a)(-3 - b)$

$= 27 + 9(a + b + c) + 3(ab + bc + ca) + abc.$

$t = 27 - 27 + 12 + 11 = 23$

Problem 29. Solution: 86.

If r_1, r_2, r_3, and r_4 are the four roots, then for some pairing of the roots, $r_1 r_2 = -32$, and then

$$r_3 r_4 = \frac{r_1 r_2 r_3 r_4}{r_1 r_2} = \frac{-1984}{-32} = 62.$$

Consequently, for some p and q,

$$x^4 - 18x^3 + kx^2 + 200x - 1984 \equiv (x - r_1)(x - r_2)(x - r_3)(x - r_4)$$

$$= (x^2 - px - 32)(x^2 - qx + 62).$$

Equating like coefficients on both sides of the identity, we find

$$p + q = 18, \qquad -62p + 32q = 200, \quad \text{and} \quad k = 62 + pq - 32.$$

Solving the first two equations for p, q, we get $p = 4$, $q = 14$. Finally,

$k = 62 + 4 \cdot 14 - 32 = 86.$

1. BASIC KNOWLEDGE

In Diophantine equations, the unknown variables are restricted to be integers.

1.1. Principles for Linear Diophantine Equations

Principle 1: A basic linear Diophantine equation is in the form:

$$ax + by = c \tag{1}$$

where a, b, and c are all integers, and a and b have a greatest common divisor d.

If d does not divide c, then this equation has no integer solutions. However if d divides c, then the general solution is:

$$(x_0 + \frac{bt}{d}, \ y_0 - \frac{at}{d}),$$ where t is integer, x_0 and y_0 are a solution to equation (1)

Principle 2: If a and b are relatively prime, there must be integers x and y, such that $ax + by = 1$.

Principle 3: If a and b are relatively prime, and c is an integer, $ax + by = c$ must have integer solutions.

Principle 4: If $x = x_0$, $y = y_0$ are a set of integer solutions of $ax + by = c$ (where a, b are positive integers, c is an integer), then all the solutions to this equation are in the form
$x = x_0 + bt$, $y = y_0 - at$ (t is an integer).

Principle 5: For equations in the form $ax + by + cz = d$, let $gcd \ (a, \ b, \ c) = e$. If e divides d (d/e = integer), then the equation has integer solutions.

1.2. Principles for fractional Diophantine Equations

Principle 1: The number of distinct pairs of positive integers (x, y) solutions for the equation $\dfrac{1}{x} + \dfrac{1}{y} = \dfrac{1}{n}$ is $N = d(n^2)$, where d is the number of factors of n^2.

Principle 2: The number of distinct pairs of positive integers (x, y) solutions where $x \neq y$ for the equation $\dfrac{1}{x} + \dfrac{1}{y} = \dfrac{1}{n}$ is $N = d(n^2) - 1$.

Principle 3: The number of ways to express $\dfrac{1}{n}$ as the sum of two positive fractions $\dfrac{1}{a}$ and $\dfrac{1}{b}$ is $\left\lceil \dfrac{d}{2} \right\rceil$, where d is the number of factors of n^2.

The symbol $\lceil \ \rceil$ is the ceiling function.

Note that the order of a and b does not matter.

Principle 4: For $\dfrac{1}{x} + \dfrac{1}{y} = \dfrac{1}{n}$, solve for x and y to get:

$$x = \frac{ny}{y-n} = n + \frac{n^2}{y-n} \text{ and } y - n \text{ is a factor of } n^2.$$

Principle 5: For $\dfrac{1}{x} + \dfrac{1}{y} = \dfrac{m}{n}$, where $m < n$, solve for x and y to get:

$$x = \frac{ny}{my-n} \text{ and } my - n \text{ is a factor of } n^2.$$

Principle 6: For equation: $\dfrac{1}{x} + \dfrac{1}{y} + \dfrac{1}{z} = \dfrac{m}{n}$, where $m < n$,

To solve this equation for x, y, and z, we first determine the range for x.

Assume that $x \le y \le z$:

$$\frac{1}{x}+\frac{1}{x}+\frac{1}{x} \ge \frac{m}{n} > \frac{1}{x} \text{ or } \frac{3}{x} \ge \frac{m}{n} > \frac{1}{x}.$$

The range for x : $\left\lceil \dfrac{n}{m} \right\rceil \le x \le \left\lfloor \dfrac{3n}{m} \right\rfloor$.

After x is determined,

$$\frac{1}{x}+\frac{1}{y}+\frac{1}{z} = \frac{m}{n} \text{ becomes } \frac{1}{y}+\frac{1}{z} = \frac{m}{n}-\frac{1}{x} \ ,$$

and we can now follow Principle 5.

1.3. Method to solve $ax + by = cxy$ $(abc \ne 0)$ Diophantine Equations

Multiplying c by both sides of equation $ax + by = cxy$:

$$cax + cby = c^2xy \qquad \Rightarrow \qquad (cx - b)(cy - a) = ab$$

2. SKILLS FOR SOLVING DIOPHANTINE EQUATIONS

2.1 Solving Linear Diophantine Equations

Example 1. Write the number 100 as the sum of two positive integers, where one of the two is divisible by 7 and the other one is divisible by 11. What is the smaller number?

Solution: 44.
Method 1:

$$7x + 11y = 100 \qquad \Rightarrow \qquad 7x = 100 - 11y \quad \Rightarrow \quad x = 12 - y + \frac{4(4-y)}{7}$$

Since x is an integer, we have $(4 - y) = 0 \quad \Rightarrow y = 4, x = 8$. The smaller number is 44.

Method 2:

$7x + 11y = 100$ $\Rightarrow$ $4y \equiv 16 \pmod 7$

$y = 4$; $x = 8$. The smaller number is 44.

Example 2. Bob's piggy bank has \$24.55 with exactly 200 coins consisting of n nickels, d dimes, and q quarters. Note that n, d, or q can be zero. Find the difference between the largest and smallest number of quarters possible in Bob's piggy bank.

Solution: 41.

$n + d + q = 200$ (1)

$5n + 10d + 25q = 2455 \Rightarrow n + 2d + 5q = 491$ (2)

$(1) \times 5 - (2)$: $4n + 3d = 509$ (3)

$3d \equiv 1$ mod 4 $\Rightarrow$ $d \equiv 3$ mod 4

The smallest value of d is 3. So the greatest value of q is 72 (with $d = 3$ and $n = 125$).

We try to get the greatest value for d by letting $n = 1$ in (4). However, we see $4 \times 1 + 3d = 509$ and d is not an integer. So we try $n = 2$. $4 \times 3 + 3d = 509$ and d = 167. So the smallest of q is 31 (with $d = 167$ and $n = 2$).

The answer is then $72 - 31 = 41$.

Note: if we do $(2) - (1)$: $d + 4q = 291$ or $(2) - (1) \times 2$: $n + 91 = 3q$ (the coefficient of one variable is 1), it will be hard to get the greatest value for d.

2.2. Solving fractional Diophantine Equations

Example 3. (NC Math Contest) How many ordered pairs (m, n) of positive integers are solutions to $\dfrac{4}{m} + \dfrac{2}{n} = 1$?

Solution: 4.

Since m and n must both be positive, it follows that $n > 2$ and $m > 4$.

$\dfrac{4}{m} + \dfrac{2}{n} = 1$ can be written as: $(m - 4)(n - 2) = 8$.

We only need to find all the ways of writing 8 as a product of positive integers. The 4 ways are (1, 8), (2, 4), (4, 2), and (8, 1) corresponding to 4 solutions, (m, n) = (5,10), (6,6), (8, 4), and (12, 3).

Example 4. Jerry started to work for one day on a project and left for vacation. Bill took over and continued to work on the project for another day. In these two days, 4/7 of the project was completed. If Bill were to work on the project alone, how many days would it take for him to finish the project if he is slower than Jerry?

Solution: 14 days.
Let x be the number of days would it take for Jerry to finish the project alone and y be the number of days would it take for Jerry to finish the project alone.

$$\frac{1}{x} + \frac{1}{y} = \frac{4}{7} \quad \Rightarrow \quad 4xy - 7x - 7y = 0 \tag{1}$$

Multiplying (1) by 4:
$$(4x - 7)(4y - 7) = 49 \tag{2}$$

We know that $y > x$. So we have:
$$\begin{cases} 4x - 7 = 1 \\ 4y - 7 = 49 \end{cases}$$

Solving we get $x = 2$ and $y = 14$.

Example 5: (IMO long listed problems) Find the triples of positive integers $x, y,$ and z satisfying $\frac{1}{x} + \frac{1}{y} + \frac{1}{z} = \frac{4}{5}$.

Solution: (2, 4, 20), and (2, 5, 10).
We let $x \le y \le z$ and we get $\frac{1}{x} + \frac{1}{x} + \frac{1}{x} \ge \frac{4}{5} > \frac{1}{x}$ or $\frac{3}{x} \ge \frac{4}{5} > \frac{1}{x}$.

From this equation, we can determine the range for x: $2 \le x \le 3$.

Case I. $x = 2$. The original equation becomes $\dfrac{1}{2} + \dfrac{1}{y} + \dfrac{1}{z} = \dfrac{4}{5}$ or $\dfrac{1}{y} + \dfrac{1}{z} = \dfrac{4}{5} - \dfrac{1}{2}$ or

$\dfrac{1}{y} + \dfrac{1}{z} = \dfrac{3}{10}$ $\Rightarrow$ $y = \dfrac{10z}{3z - 10}$.

$3z - 10$ must be a factor of $10^2 = 2^2 \times 5^2$ or one of the factors: 1, 2, 4, 5, 10, 20, 25, 50, and 100.

Only $3z - 10 = 2$ and $3z - 10 = 5$ give integer values z, so we have the solutions (2, 4, 20) and (2, 5, 10).

Case II. $x = 3$. The original equation becomes $\dfrac{1}{y} + \dfrac{1}{z} = \dfrac{4}{5} - \dfrac{1}{3}$ or $\dfrac{1}{y} + \dfrac{1}{z} = \dfrac{7}{15}$

We get $y = \dfrac{15z}{7z - 15}$, where $7z - 15$ is a factor of $15^2 = 3^2 \times 5^2$, or one of the

following factors: 1, 3, 5, 9, 15, 25, 45, 75, or 225.

We set $7z - 15$ to be the values of these factors, but after going through each factor, we see that z is not an integer for any of the factors.

So we have the solutions (2, 4, 20) and (2, 5, 10).

Example 6: Alex bought n math books with d dollars, where d is a positive integer. He sold two books at half their cost and the rest of books at a profit of \$9 per book. Find the value of d if he bought the least possible number of books and still made a profit of \$81.

Solution: 108.

We are given that Alex paid d dollars for n book, and so for each book he paid d/n

dollars. Therefore, he made $2 \times \dfrac{1}{2} \times \dfrac{d}{n}$ on the two books he sold to the school, and

$(n - 2)(\dfrac{d}{n} + 9)$ on the rest of the books.

So we have $(n - 2)\left(\dfrac{d}{n} + 9\right) + 2\dfrac{d}{2n} = d + 81$ $\Rightarrow 9n - \dfrac{d}{n} = 99$ $\Rightarrow d = 9n(n - 11)$.

The least possible value of n is 12. We let $n = 12$ and we get $d = 108$.

2.3. The Method of Factoring

Example 7. (2000 Mathcounts National Sprint) The product of a two-digit number and 5 is equal to the product of the same two-digit number with its digits reversed and 6. What is the sum of the digits of the number?

Solution: 9.

$5(10a + b) = 6(10b + a)$

$50a + 5b = 60\, b + 6a$

$44a - 55b = 0 \qquad \Rightarrow \qquad 4a = 5b.$

Since 4 and 5 are relatively prime, so we get $a - 5$ and $b - 4$. The sum is 9.

Example 8. (1998 Mathcounts National Sprint #29) Great Aunt Minnie's age plus the square of Great Uncle Paul's age is 7308. Great Uncle Paul's age plus the square of Great Aunt Minnie's age is 6974. What is the sum of Great Uncle Paul's age and Great Aunt Minnie's age?

Solution: 168.

We are given that

$$M + P^2 = 7308 \qquad\qquad\qquad (1)$$
$$M^2 + P = 6974 \qquad\qquad\qquad (2)$$

$(1) - (2)$: $P^2 - M^2 + M - P = 334$

$\Rightarrow (P - M)(P + M) - (P - M) = 334$

$\Rightarrow (P - M)(P + M - 1) = 2 \times 167.$

$P + M - 1 = 167 \Rightarrow P + M = 168.$

Example 9. Find n, the number of all positive integer solutions to the equation $x^2 - y^2 + 2y - 56 = 0.$

Solution: 2.

Completing the square yields

$$x^2 - (y-1)^2 = 55 \quad \Rightarrow \quad (x+y-1)(x-y+1) = 55.$$

We know that $x+y-1 \geq x-y+1$, $x+y-1$ and $x-y+1$ have the same parity, and $x-y+1 > 0$,

$$\begin{cases} x+y-1 = 55 \\ x-y+1 = 1 \end{cases} \quad \Rightarrow \quad x = 28; \quad y = 28$$

$$\begin{cases} x+y-1 = 11 \\ x-y+1 = 5 \end{cases} \quad \Rightarrow \quad x = 8; \quad y = 4$$

Therefore, the two solutions for (x, y) are $(28, 28)$ and $(8, 4)$.

Example 10. Find n, the number of all nonnegative integer solutions to the equation $xyz + xy + xz + yz + x + y + z = 213$.

Solution: 9.

The given equation can be written as $(x+1)(y+1)(z+1) = 214$.

$214 = 1 \times 1 \times 214 = 1 \times 2 \times 107$

Without loss of generality, let $x \geq y \geq z$

$$\begin{cases} x+1 = 214 \\ y+1 = 1 \\ z+1 = 1 \end{cases} \quad \Rightarrow \quad x = 213, \quad y = 0, \quad z = 0$$

$$\begin{cases} x+1 = 107 \\ y+1 = 2 \\ z+1 = 1 \end{cases} \quad \Rightarrow \quad x = 106, \quad y = 1, \quad z = 0$$

Based on the property of symmetry, we have all the solutions of (x, y, z):

$(213, 0, 0)$, $(0, 213, 0)$, $(0, 0, 213)$;

$(106, 1, 0)$, $(106, 0, 1)$, $(1, 106, 0)$, $(1, 0, 106)$, $(0, 106, 1)$, $(0, 1, 106)$.

There are a total of 9.

Example 11. Find $56x^2y^2$ if x and y are positive integers such that $3y^2 + 4x^2y^2 - 8x^2 = 139$.

Solution: 2016.

$$3y^2 + 4x^2y^2 - 8x^2 = 139 \qquad \Rightarrow \qquad (y^2 - 2)(4x^2 + 3) = 7 \times 19$$

Since $4x^2 + 3 \geq 7$, we have two cases:

Case 1:
$$\begin{cases} 4x^2 + 3 = 19 \\ y^2 - 2 = 7 \end{cases}$$
This gives us $x^2 = 4$ and $y^2 = 9$.

Case 2:
$$\begin{cases} 4x^2 + 3 = 7 \\ y^2 - 2 = 19 \end{cases}$$
There are no positive integer solutions for case 2.

$56\, x^2y^2 = 56 \times 36 = 2016$.

Example 12. Find all positive integer solutions for $4x^2 - 4xy - 3y^2 - 4x + 10y - 16 = 0$.

Solution: $(6, 4)$.

The given equation can be factored into

$(2x - 3y + 1)(2x + y - 3) = 13$.

We then have

$2x - 3y + 1 = 1$

$2x + y - 3 = 13$;

Or

$2x - 3y + 1 = 13$

$2x + y - 3 = 1$.

Solving we get: $x = 6$ and $y = 4$; and $x = 3$ and $y = -2$.

Since x and y are positive, the solution is $(6, 4)$.

Example 13. How many pairs of integer solutions are there for $3x^2 + 2y^2 - 12x - 8y + 30 = 0$?

Solution: 1.

Completing the squares: $3(x-2)^2 + 2(y-3)^2 = 0$.

The only solution is $x = 2$ and $y = 3$.

Example 14. Solve the equation $x^2 - 2y^2 = 1$ if both x and y are prime numbers.

Solution: (3, 2).

Since $2y^2$ is even, x^2 must be odd and x must be odd.

The given equation can be written as $y^2 = \dfrac{x^2 - 1}{2} = \dfrac{(x-1)(x+1)}{2}$.

We know that $x + 1$ and $x - 1$ have the same parity and they must be even. Thus y^2 must be even and y must be even.

The only even prime number is 2. So $y = 2$ and then $x = 3$.

2.4. Using Inequalities

Example 15. (1998 Mathcounts National Sprint #29) Great Aunt Minnie's age plus the square of Great Uncle Paul's age is 7308. Great Uncle Paul's age plus the square of Great Aunt Minnie's age is 6974. What is the sum of Great Uncle Paul's age and Great Aunt Minnie's age?

Solution: 168.

We are given that

$$M + P^2 = 7308 \tag{1}$$

$$M^2 + P = 6974 \tag{2}$$

Since P and M are both positive integers, from (1), we know that $P \leq 85$ and from (2), we know that $M \leq 83$.

Substitute the value of P, 85, into (1), to get $M = 83$.

$P = 85$ and $M = 83$ also satisfies equation (2), so the answer is $85 + 83 = 168.$

Example 16. Find n, the number of all integer solutions to the equation $5x^2 + 2y^2 = 98$.

Solution: 6.

Since $5x^2 + 2y^2 = 98$, we know that $5x^2 \leq 100$ $\Rightarrow$ $x^2 \leq 20$.

$5x^2$ must be even since it equals $98 - 2y^2$, so x^2 can only be 0, 4, or 16.

This gives the values for y^2 as $y^2 = 7^2$, $y^2 = 39$, and $y^2 = 3^2$.

Notice that 39 is not a square number, so the desired solutions for (x, y) are: (0,7), (0, -7), (4, 3), (4, -3), (-4, 3), and (-4, -3).

Example 17. Find all triples of positive integers (x, y, z) such that $xy + yz + zx - xyz = 2$.

Solution: (2, 3, 4), (2, 4, 3), (3, 2, 4), (3, 4, 2), (4, 2, 3), (4, 3, 2), (1, 1, 1).

Method 1:

Let $u = x - 1$, $v = y - 1$, $w = z - 1$. The equation becomes $u + v + w = uvw$. We either have $(u, v, w) = (0, 0, 0)$ or $uvw \neq 0$. In the latter case the equation is equivalent to $1/vw + 1/wu + 1/uv = 1$, which is of the type $1/m + 1/n + 1/p = 1$. Assuming $m \leq n \leq p$, we obtain the solutions $(m, n, p) = (2, 3, 6), (2, 4, 4), (3, 3, 3)$. The last two situations are not possible, since then $(uvw)^2$ would equal 32 and 27, respectively, which are not perfect squares.

Thus, we have $vw = 2$, $wu = 3$, $uv = 6$, which gives us $uvw = 6$.

It follows that $u = 3$, $v = 2$, $w = 1$.

The solutions (x, y, z) are $(1, 1, 1)$ and all the permutations of $(4, 3, 2)$.

Method 2:

From the equation it follows that $xy + yz + zx > xyz$; hence $1/x + 1/y + 1/z > 1$. Assuming that $x \leq y \leq z$, from the last relation we obtain $3x > 1$, that is, $x \in \{1, 2\}$.

If $x = 1$, then the equation becomes $y + z = 2$; hence $y = z = 1$, giving the solution $(1, 1, 1)$.

If $x = 2$, then the equation is equivalent to $2y + 2z - yz = 2$; hence $(y - 2)(z - 2) = 2$, giving the solution $(2, 3, 4)$, and all the permutations of $(2, 3, 4)$.

2.5. The Method of Modular Arithmetic

Example 18. (Mathcounts 1988 National Team#10) A developer has 87 acres and he would like to divide it into smaller lots. Some should be 2 acres, some should be 3 acres, and some should be 5 acres. If the developer must have exactly 25 lots (allowing no fractional parts of lots), and at least one lot of each type, how many different ways can he divide up the 87 acres?

Solution: 6.

$$x + y + z = 25 \qquad\qquad (1)$$
$$2x + 3y + 5z = 87 \qquad\qquad (2)$$

First we eliminate z, the variable with the largest coefficient to obtain,

$3x + 2y = 38 \qquad \Rightarrow 2y = 38 - 3x \qquad \Rightarrow 38 - 3x \equiv 0 \qquad (\text{mod } 2)$

x can range from 2 (the smallest value) to 12 (the greatest value). There are a total of 6 values for x, and there are 6 corresponding values for y and z. The solution is: 6 ways.

Example 19. (1995 Mathcounts National Sprint Round #15) Suppose a coin purse contains 30 coins which are either nickels, dimes, and/or quarters. How many different combinations of these coins are there whose value is $5?

Solution: 4.

Let n be number of nickels, d be number of dimes, and q be number of quarters. According to the problem,

$n + d + q = 30 \qquad\qquad (1)$

$$5n + 10d + 25q = 500 \qquad\qquad (2)$$

The question stated that q can be zero; however, if q is zero, 30 coins of dimes and nickels are not enough to make $5.00, so none of n, d, or q is zero. Multiplying equation (1) by 5 and subtract the result from (2) yields

$$d + 4q = 70 \qquad\qquad (3)$$

From (3) we can deduce that q must be less than 18 and $d \equiv 2 \pmod 4$

If $d = 2$, then $q = 17$ and $n = 11$ (from (1))
If $d = 6$, then $q = 16$ and $n = 8$
If $d = 10$, then $q = 15$ and $n = 5$
If $d = 14$, then $q = 14$ and $n = 2$
If $d = 18$, then $q = 13$ and $n = -2$ (not possible).
So we can conclude that there are 4 different combinations.

Example 20. Let $2x + 3y = 72$. How many ordered pairs (x, y), where x and y are whole numbers, will satisfy the equation?   (2002 Mathcounts National).

Solution: 13.
Note that both x and y are whole numbers, which means that they can be zero, so we are trying to find all non-negative solutions.

Re-write the equation as $72 - 2x \equiv 0 \mod 3$
The largest value of x could be 36, and the smallest value of x could be zero.

So $36 = 0 + (n - 1) \times 3$ and $n = 13$. So there are 13 values for x, then 13 values for y. Total 13 ordered pairs.

Example 21. (Mathcounts Competitions) In how many ways can a debt of $69 be paid exactly using only 5-dollar and 2-dollar bills?

Solution: 7.

$5x + 2y = 69$

$69 - 5x \equiv 0 \mod 2$

$1 - x \equiv 0 \qquad \mod 2$

$x = 1 \qquad \mod 2$

The smallest value for x is 1 and the greatest possible value is 13. There are 7 ways.

$(x = 1, 3, 5, 7, 9, 11, 13.)$

Example 22. (1998 Mathcounts National Team #3) Exactly one ordered pair of positive integers (x, y) satisfies the equation $37 x + 73 y = 2016$. What is the sum of $x + y$?

Solution: 36.

$2016 - 73y \equiv 0 \qquad \mod 37$

$18 + y \equiv 0 \qquad \mod 37$

$y \equiv -18 \equiv 19 \qquad \mod 37$

$x = 17.$

$x + y = 17 + 19 = 36.$

2.6. The Decomposition Method

Example 23. Some balls are putting into at least 10 boxes. The number of balls in each box is the same. If each box has 12 balls, there is one ball left over. If the number of boxes is increased by 3, there is no ball left over. Find the number of balls.

Solution: 385.

Let x be the number of boxes at first and $x + 3$ be the number of boxes in the end, y be the number of balls in each box with $x + 3$ boxes.

$$12x + 1 = (x + 3)y \qquad \Rightarrow \qquad y = 12 - \frac{35}{x+3}.$$

We know that $x \geq 10$ and 35 is divisible by $x + 3$. So $x = 32$ and $y = 11$. The number of balls is $35 \times 11 = 385$.

Example 24. How many pairs of positive integer solutions are there for the equation $2(x + y) = xy + 7$?

Solution: 2.

The given equation can be written as $y = \dfrac{2x - 7}{x - 2} = 2 - \dfrac{3}{x - 2}$.

Since we want to find the positive integer solutions, we see that $(x - 2)$ must be a factor of 3.

$x - 2 = 1 \qquad \Rightarrow \qquad x = 3$ and $y = -1$ (ignored since y must be positive).

$x - 2 = 3 \qquad \Rightarrow \qquad x = 5$ and $y = 1$.

$x - 2 = -1 \qquad \Rightarrow \qquad x = 1$ and $y = 5$.

$x - 2 = -3 \qquad \Rightarrow \qquad x = -1$ (ignored since x must be positive).

Example 25. Find n, the number of all integer solutions to the equation $2xy - 2x^2 + 3x - 5y + 11 = 0$.

Solution: 4.

$2xy - 2x^2 + 3x - 5y + 11 = 0 \qquad \Rightarrow \qquad y = \dfrac{2x^2 - 3x - 11}{2x - 5} = x + 1 - \dfrac{6}{2x - 5}$

Since y is integer, $\dfrac{6}{2x - 5}$ must also be an integer.

Since $2x - 5$ is odd, $2x - 5$ must be also have an odd factor of 6, so we have:
$2x - 5 = \pm 1;\ 2x - 5 = \pm 3$.
$x = 3, 2, 4$ and 1. The corresponding values for y are $-2, 9, 3$, and 4.

The solutions for (x, y) are $(3, -2)$, $(2, 9)$, $(4, 3)$, and $(1, 4)$.

Example 26. (AIME) Find $3x^2y^2$ if x and y are integers such that $y^2 + 3x^2y^2 = 30x^2 + 517$.

Solution: 588.

Method 1 (our solution):

$$y^2 = \frac{30x^2 + 517}{3x^2 + 1} = \frac{30x^2 + 10 + 507}{3x^2 + 1} = 10 + \frac{507}{3x^2 + 1} = 10 + \frac{3 \times 13^2}{3x^2 + 1}$$

We know that $3x^2 + 1 \geq 4$, so $3x^2 + 1$ can be the following values: 13, 3×13, 13^2, 3×13^2. Solve for x in each case, and the only integer answers are $x = 2$ and $x = 4$. When $x = 2$, the value of $y = 7$. When $x = 4$, we get no integral value for y. Therefore $3x^2y^2 = 588$.

Method 2 (official solution):

Rewrite the given equation in the form $(y^2 - 10)(3x^2 + 1) = 3 \cdot 13^2$, and note that, since y is an integer and $3x^2 + 1$ is a positive integer, $y^2 - 10$ must be a positive integer. Consequently, $y^2 - 10 = 1, 3, 13, 39, 169$ or 507, implying that $y^2 = 11$, 13, 23, 49, 179 or 517. Since the only perfect square in the second list is 49, it follows that $y^2 - 10 = 39$, implying that $3x^2 + 1 = 13$, $x^2 = 4$ and $3x^2y^2 = 12 \cdot 49 = 588$.

2.7. The Parity Method

Example 27. How many prime numbers of x and y satisfy the equation $x^2 - 2y^2 = 1$?

Solution: 1.

From $x^2 = 2y^2 + 1$, we know that x^2 is odd and x is also odd.

Let $x = 2n + 1$, where n is positive integer.

The original equation can be written as $(2n + 1)^2 = 2y^2 + 1$, or $y^2 = 2(n^2 + n)$.

So we know that y is even. Since y is prime, $y = 2$.

Substituting $y = 2$ into the original equation, we get $x = 3$.

Therefore the prime solutions are $x = 3$, $y = 2$.

2.8. The Discriminant method

Example 28. How many ordered pairs of integers (x, y) satisfy $\dfrac{x+y}{x^2 - xy + y^2} = \dfrac{3}{7}$?

Solution: $\begin{cases} x = 5, \\ y = 4, \end{cases} \begin{cases} x = 4, \\ y = 5. \end{cases}$

The given equation can be written as $3x^2 - 3xy + 3y^2 - 7x - 7y = 0$ or
$3x^2 - (3y + 7)x + 3y^2 - 7y = 0$.

Since x is integer, we have $\Delta = (3y + 7)^2 - 12(3y^2 - 7y) \geq 0$ or
$27y^2 - 126y - 49 \leq 0$.

It follows that $\dfrac{21 - 14\sqrt{3}}{9} \leq y \leq \dfrac{21 + 14\sqrt{3}}{9}$.

Since y is an integer, $y = 0, 1, 2, 3, 4, 5$.

All the solutions are: $\begin{cases} x = 5, \\ y = 4, \end{cases} \begin{cases} x = 4, \\ y = 5. \end{cases}$

PROBLEMS

Problem 1. Find the number of solution-pairs in positive integers of the equation $3x + 5y = 501$.

Problem 2. Find the number of solution-pairs in positive integers of the equation $4x + 5y = 98$.

Problem 3. Find the number of possible positive integer values of k such that the equation $kx - 12 = 3k$ has an integral solution.

Problem 4. If n is the number of ways that 10 dollars can be changed into dimes and quarters, with at least one of each coin being used, what is n?

Problem 5. Solving for integers: $\begin{cases} 5x + 7y + 2z = 24, \\ 3x - y - 4z = 4. \end{cases}$

Problem 6. In the xy-plane, find the number of lines whose x-intercept is a positive prime number and whose y-intercept is a positive integer that pass through the point $(4, 3)$.

Problem 7. Find the smallest positive value of $x + y + z$, where x, y, and z are different positive integers that satisfy this equation: $\dfrac{1}{x} + \dfrac{1}{y} + \dfrac{1}{z} = \dfrac{7}{10}$.

Problem 8. Find the positive integer value of n that satisfy this equation: $\dfrac{1}{n} + \dfrac{1}{n+1} + \dfrac{1}{n+2} + \dfrac{1}{n+3} = \dfrac{19}{20}$.

Problem 9. Find the number of solution-pairs in integers of the equation

$(x+1)^2 + (y-2)^2 = 1$.

Problem 10. . Find the number of solution-pairs in positive integers of the equation $x^2 + 72 = y^2$.

Problem 11. The product of three prime numbers is the same as eleven times their sum. What is the largest possible value of the three prime numbers?

Problem 12. Find all integer solutions to $x^2 - 5xy + 6y^2 - 3x + 5y - 11 = 0$.

Problem 13. Find all positive integer solutions to $4x^2 - 4xy - 3y^2 = 21$.

Problem 14. (AMC) The number of triples (a, b, c) of positive integers which satisfy the simultaneous equations
$$ab + bc = 44,$$
$$ac + bc = 23,$$
is
(A) 0   (B) 1   (C) 2   (D) 3   (E) 4

Problem 15. Find two integers such that the sum of the sum, the difference, the product, and the quotient is 450.

Problem 16. (NC Math Contest) Find the sum of all positive integers n so that $2001 + n^2$ will be a perfect square.

Problem 17. Find the number of solutions in positive integers of $2x + 3y = 763$.

Problem 18. Find the positive integer solutions of the equation $2x + 3y + 5z = 15$.

Problem 19. Find all pairs (x, y) of integers such that $x^3 + y^3 = (x + y)^2$.

Problem 20. Solve in positive integers the equation $3(xy + yz + zx) = 4xyz$.

Problem 21. (AMC) Find the number of pairs (m, n) of integers which satisfy the equation $m^3 + 6m^2 + 5m = 27n^3 + 9n^2 + 9n + 1$.
(A) 0   (B) 1   (C) 3   (D) 9   (E) infinitely many

Problem 22. (AIME) What is the smallest positive integer that can be expressed as the sum of nine consecutive integers, the sum of ten consecutive integers, and the sum of eleven consecutive integers?

Problem 23. Find the number of positive integers k such that $kx - 72 = 3k$ has an integer solution for x.

Problem 24. Find one set of integer solutions to $x^2 - 51y^2 = 1$.

Problem 25. How many ordered pairs of integers (x, y) satisfy $x + y = x^2 - xy + y^2$?

Problem 26. (Russian Mathematical Olympiad) Find the positive integer solutions to the equation $x^3 - y^3 = xy + 61$.

SOLUTIONS

Problem 1. Solution: 33.

Method 1:

The given equation is equivalent to $y = 3(167 - x)/5$. For y to be a positive integer, $(167 - x)$ must be a positive multiple of 5; this is the case for the 33 positive integers $x = 5k + 2$, $k = 0, 1, 2, \cdots, 32$.

Method 2:

We use the theorem stating that $(x, y) = (x_0 - bt, y_0 + at)$ gives all solutions in integers of the equation $ax + by = c$ if a and b are relatively prime integers and (x_0, y_0) is any particular solution, the different integers t giving the different solutions. The theorem applies to the present equation $3x + 5y = 501$ with a particular solution $(x_0, y_0) = (167, 0)$ and all solutions are given by $(x, y) = (167 - 5t, 0 + 3t)$. The integers $t = 1, 2, 3, \cdots, 33$ give all 33 solutions in which both x and y are positive, and only those solutions.

Method 3:

$3x + 5y = 501 \implies \quad y \equiv 0 \bmod 3$

So $y = 3, 6, \ldots 99$. The number of values for y is $(99 - 3) 3 + 1 = 33$.

Problem 2. Solution: 5.

y must be even and $y \leq 19$. So the possible values for y are 2, 4, 6, 8, 10, 12, 14, 16, and 18.

When y is a multiple 4, the left hand side of the equation is a multiple of 4 but the right hand side is not. So y must be in the form of $4k + 2$. So $y = 2, 6, 10, 14, 18$. We can check that when $y = 2, 6, 10, 14, 18$, the values of x are all positive integers. So the answer is 5.

Problem 3. Solution: 6.

The given equation can be written as $x = \dfrac{12}{k} + 3$. k must be a factor of 12. We know that 12 has 6 factors: 1, 2, 3, 4, 6, 12. So k must be one of them. The answer is 6.

Problem 4. Solution: 19.

Method 1:

Let q and d denote the number of quarters and dimes, respectively, to total $10. Then, in cents, $25q + 10d = 1000$, which is equivalent to $2d = 2(40 - q)$. Since the left side is a positive even integer, the right side must also be a positive even integer, so $40 - q$ must be even and positive. This is the case when q is any even integer less than 40, so the number n of solutions is 19 or choice (E).

Method 2 :

Let q and d denote the number of quarters and dimes, respectively. Then we can write the equation where the unit is in cents:

$25q + 10d = 1000$, or $5q + 2d = 200$.

$\Rightarrow \quad 200 - 5q \equiv 0 \pmod 2$.

Since both q and d cannot be zero, then $2 - q \equiv 0 \pmod 2$

$q = 2$, and $d = 95$.

Also, recall that the general solution to such an equation is: $q = q_0 + 2t = 2 + 2t$, and $d = d_0 - 5t = 95 - 5t$

Because $95 - 5t \geq 1 \Rightarrow \quad t \leq 18.8 = 18$ we know that t is from 0 to 18, so n is 19.

Method 3:

First, move the term with larger coefficient (or the one we want to solve for) to the right hand side of the equation.

$5q + 2d = 200 \Rightarrow 2d = 200 - 5q \Rightarrow 200 - 5q \equiv 0 \pmod 2$.

From this equation, we see that the largest q is 40.

We then obtain the smallest q by reducing both 200 and 5 module 2: $2 - q \equiv 0$. The smallest q is 2.

Because this is in mod 2, q can be 2, 4, 6, 8, 10, 12,..., 40. There are 20 values. Finally, we must check the two extreme values, when $q = 2$ and 40. When $q = 40$, we see that $d = 0$, which cannot be possible, so we must reduce the number of quarters in use.

If we reduce the number of quarters by two, that is, if we use 38 quarters, d will be a valid amount. Then the total number of ways will be $n = 19$.

Problem 5. Solutions:

We eliminate z in $\begin{cases} 5x + 7y + 2z = 24, \\ 3x - y - 4z = 4. \end{cases}$:

$13x + 13y = 52$, or $x + y = 4$.

We observe that one solution to the equation $x + y = 4$ is $x_0 = 0$, $y_0 = 4$.

So the general solutions are $\begin{cases} x = t, \\ y = 4 - t. \end{cases}$ (t is integer)

Substituting into $5x + 7y + 2z = 24$ we get $z = -2 + t$.

Therefore the general solution is $\begin{cases} x = t, \\ y = 4 - t, \\ z = -2 + t \end{cases}$ (t is integer).

Problem 6. Solution: 2.

Method 1:

The equation of the line with intercepts $(a, 0)$ and $(0, b)$ is: $\dfrac{x}{a} + \dfrac{y}{b} = 1$ (1)

Since the line passes through (4, 3), (1) can be written as $\dfrac{4}{a}+\dfrac{3}{b}=1$ (2)

Solving for b in equation (2):

$$b=\dfrac{3a}{a-4}=3+\dfrac{12}{a-4}$$

Since b is a positive integer, $a-4$ must be a factor of 12. Since a is prime, the only values for a are $a=5$ and $a=7$. So we have two lines.

Method 2:

The equation of the line with intercepts $(a, 0)$ and $(0, b)$ is: $\dfrac{x}{a}+\dfrac{y}{b}=1$ (1)

Since the line passes through (4, 3), (1) can be written as $\dfrac{4}{a}+\dfrac{3}{b}=1$ (2)

(2) becomes: $ab-3a-4b=0$ $\Rightarrow$ $(a-4)(b-3)=12$.

We have

$a-4=1$ and $b-3=12$ $\Rightarrow$ $a=5$ and $b=15$.

or $a-4=2$ and $b-3=6$ $\Rightarrow$ $a=6$ and $b=9$

or $a-4=3$ and $b-3=4$ $\Rightarrow$ $a=7$ and $b=7$.

a can also be 15 or 9. Since a is a prime number, we have two values for a (5 and 7).

Problem 7. Solution: 14.

We let $x\le y\le z$ and we get $\dfrac{1}{x}+\dfrac{1}{x}+\dfrac{1}{x}\ge\dfrac{7}{10}>\dfrac{1}{x}$ or $\dfrac{3}{x}\ge\dfrac{7}{10}>\dfrac{1}{x}$

The range for x is: $\dfrac{30}{7}\ge x>\dfrac{10}{7}$.

So we have $2\le x\le4$.

Case I. If $x=2$,

$$\dfrac{1}{2}+\dfrac{1}{y}+\dfrac{1}{z}=\dfrac{7}{10} \Rightarrow \dfrac{1}{y}+\dfrac{1}{z}=\dfrac{7}{10}-\dfrac{1}{2}=\dfrac{1}{5} \Rightarrow \dfrac{1}{y}+\dfrac{1}{z}=\dfrac{1}{5}$$

Since we only need to find out the smallest value of $x + y + z$, we only need to try to find values of y and z as close as possible.

Let $\dfrac{1}{y} + \dfrac{1}{z} = \dfrac{1}{5} = \dfrac{1}{10} + \dfrac{1}{10}$,

$x = 2$, $y = 10$, and $z = 10$

Since x, y, and z must be different, we can rule out this case.

Case II. $x = 3$

$\dfrac{1}{y} + \dfrac{1}{z} = \dfrac{7}{10} - \dfrac{1}{3} = \dfrac{11}{30}$

$\dfrac{1}{y} + \dfrac{1}{z} = \dfrac{11}{30} = \dfrac{5}{30} + \dfrac{6}{30} = \dfrac{1}{6} + \dfrac{1}{5}$,

$x = 3$, $y = 6$, and $z = 5$.

$x + y + z = 14$

Case III. $x = 4$

$\dfrac{1}{y} + \dfrac{1}{z} = \dfrac{7}{10} - \dfrac{1}{4} = \dfrac{9}{20} = \dfrac{4}{20} + \dfrac{5}{20} = \dfrac{1}{5} + \dfrac{1}{4}$

$x = 4$, $y = 5$, and $z = 4$

Since x, y, and z must be different, we can rule out this case. The least sum of x, y, and z is 14 from Case 2.

Problem 8. Solution: 3.

We see that $\dfrac{1}{n} > \dfrac{19}{20} \times \dfrac{1}{4} > \dfrac{1}{n+3}$.

Solving for n: $1\dfrac{4}{19} < n < 4\dfrac{4}{19}$.

Since n is an integer, $2 \leq n \leq 4$

We try $n = 2$, 3, and 4 and $n = 3$ works: $\dfrac{1}{3} + \dfrac{1}{3+1} + \dfrac{1}{3+2} + \dfrac{1}{3+3} = \dfrac{19}{20}$.

Problem 9. Solution: 4.

We know that both x and y are integers. We have

$$\begin{cases}(x+1)^2 = 0 \\ (y-2)^2 = 1\end{cases}$$

or

$$\begin{cases}(x+1)^2 = 1 \\ (y-2)^2 = 0\end{cases}$$

Solving we get $x = -1$, $y = 3$; $x = -1$, $y = 1$; $x = 0$, $y = 2$; $x = -2$, $y = 2$.

The answer is 4.

Problem 10. Solution: 3.

The given equation can be written as $y^2 - x^2 = 72 \implies (y+x)(y-x) = 72$.

We know that $72 = 1 \times 72 = 2 \times 36 = 4 \times 18 = 6 \times 12 = 8 \times 9$. We also know that $(y+x)$ and $(y-x)$ have the same parity. So the first and the last pairs will not work.

We have

$$\begin{cases}(y-x) = 2 \\ (y+x) = 36\end{cases}$$

or

$$\begin{cases}(y-x) = 2 \\ (y+x) = 18\end{cases}$$

or

$$\begin{cases}(y-x) = 6 \\ (y+x) = 12\end{cases}$$

Solving we get (3, 9), (7, 11), and (17, 19). The answer is 3.

Problem 11. Solution: 13.

Let three prime numbers be x, y, and z.

$$xyz = 11(x + y + z) \qquad (1)$$

So one of x, y, and z must be 11. Let it be z.

(1) becomes: $xy = x + y + 11 \implies$ $(x-1)(y-1) = 12 = 1 \times 12 = 2 \times 6 = 3 \times 4$

Solving we get ($x = 3$ and $y = 7$; $x = 7$ and $y = 3$; $x = 2$ and $y = 13$; $x = 13$ and $y = 2$. So three prime numbers can be (3, 7, 11) or (2, 11, 13). The answer is 13.

Problem 12. Solution: $(-22, -11)$, $(0, 1)$, $(-30, -11)$, and $(8, 1)$.

We write the given equation as $(x - 2y)(x - 3y) + (x - 3y) - 4(x - 2y) = 11$.

Thus we have $(x - 2y + 1)(x - 3y - 4) = 7$.

So $\begin{cases} x - 2y + 1 = \pm 1, \\ x - 3y - 4 = \pm 7. \end{cases}$

Solving we get: $\begin{cases} x = -22, \\ y = -11. \end{cases}$; $\begin{cases} x = 0, \\ y = 1. \end{cases}$; $\begin{cases} x = -30, \\ y = -11. \end{cases}$; or $\begin{cases} x = 8, \\ y = 1. \end{cases}$

The solutions are $(-22, -11)$, $(0, 1)$, $(-30, -11)$, and $(8, 1)$.

Problem 13. Solution:

From $4x^2 - 4xy - 3y^2 = 21$ we get $(2x + y)(2x - 3y) = 21$,

The solutions are: $\begin{cases} x = 8, \\ y = 5, \end{cases}$ and $\begin{cases} x = 3, \\ y = 1. \end{cases}$

Problem 14. Solution: (C).

Method 1 (official solution):

From the second equation, $c(a + b) = 23$ and 23 is prime. Consequently, the two factors must be 1 and 23. Since a and b are positive integers, $a + b > 1$. Hence one must have $c = 1$ and $a + b = 23$. Upon substituting 1 for c and $23 - a$ for b into the first equation, it becomes a quadratic, $a^2 - 22a + 21 = 0$, with solutions $a = 1$ and $a = 21$. Both of these, and the corresponding values of b (22 and 2), satisfy both equations. Thus the solutions are (1, 22, 1) and (21, 2, 1).

Method 2 (our solution):

From the second equation, we get $c(a + b) = 23$. Since 23 is prime and a and b are positive integers, so $a + b \geq 2$. Thus $c = 1$ and $a + b = 23$.

From the first equation, $b(a + 1) = 44 = 1 \times 44 = 2 \times 22 = 4 \times 11$.

We have:

$b = 1, a + 1 = 44$	$\Rightarrow$	$a = 43, b = 1.$
$b = 2, a + 1 = 22$	$\Rightarrow$	$a = 21, b = 2.$
$b = 4, a + 1 = 11$	$\Rightarrow$	$a = 10, b = 4.$
$b = 44, a + 1 = 1$	$\Rightarrow$	no solution.
$b = 22, a + 1 = 2$	$\Rightarrow$	$a = 1, b = 22.$
$b = 11, a + 1 = 4$	$\Rightarrow$	$a = 3, b = 11.$

Note that $a + b = 23$. The solutions are $(21, 2, 1)$, and are $(1, 22, 1)$.

Problem 15. Solution: $(28, 14), (-32, -16), (72, 4), (-108, -6), (100, 2), (-200, -4), (-900, -2)$.

Let the two integers be x and y.

We have $x + y + (x - y) + xy + \dfrac{x}{y} = 450$. $\qquad\qquad$ (1)

Since x and y are integers, $x + y$, $x - y$, xy are all integers.

From (1) we know that $\dfrac{x}{y}$ is also an integer.

(1) can be written as $\dfrac{x}{y} + 2x + xy = 450$

Or $\dfrac{x}{y}(1 + 2y + y^2) = 450$ or $\dfrac{x}{y}(1 + y)^2 = 450$ $\qquad\qquad$ (2)

We know that $450 = 1 \cdot 2 \cdot 3^2 \cdot 5^2$. So $\dfrac{x}{y}$ can only be 2, 18, 50, 450.

Therefore we can find the following solutions:

$(x, y) = (28, 14), (-32, -16), (72, 4), (-108, -6), (100, 2), (-200, -4), (-900, -2)$.

Problem 16. Solution: 1384.

$2001 + n^2 = m^2 \quad \Rightarrow \quad m^2 - n^2 = 2001$

$\Rightarrow (m+n)(m-n) = 2001 \Rightarrow (m+n)(m-n) = 3 \cdot 23 \cdot 29$

$m+n$	2001	29×23	29×3	23×3
$m-n$	1	3	23	29
n	1000	332	32	20

$\sum n = 1384.$

Problem 17. Solution: 127.
Method 1 (official solution):
Solving $2x + 3y = 763$ for x, we have

$$x = \frac{763 - 3y}{2}.$$

Since x is a positive integer, $763 - 3y$ must be a positive even number, so that y must be a positive odd integer, such that $3y \leq 763$. There are 254 multiples of 3 less than 763, half of which are even multiples and half, odd multiples. Therefore, there are 127 possible solutions to the given equation under the stated conditions.

Method 2 (our solution):
$2x + 3y = 763$ (mod 2) $\Rightarrow$ $y \equiv 1$ (mod 2)

The greatest possible value for y is $\left\lfloor \dfrac{763 - 2}{3} \right\rfloor = 253$.

Therefore y can be 1, 3, 5,..., 253. We know that $253 = 1 + (n-1)2 \Rightarrow n = 127$.

Problem 18. Solution: (1, 1, 2) and (2, 2, 1).
Since $(2, 3, 5) = 1$, the equation has solutions.
Let $u = x + 2z$. We have $2u + 3y + z = 15$.
Therefore $z = 15 - 2u - 3y$, $x = u - 2z = 5u + 6y - 30$, where u and y are any integers and $x > 0$, $z > 0$.
We then have $5u + 6y - 30 > 0$ (1)
$15 - 2u - 3y > 0$ (2)
Solving (1) and (2): $-3y + 15 > 0$.

So $0 < y < 5$, or $y = 1, 2, 3, 4$.

When $y = 1$, from (1) and (2), we get $\dfrac{24}{5} < u < 6$.

Thus $u = 5$.

From $2u + 3y + z = 15$, we get $z = 2$, so $x = 1$.

When $y = 2$, it follows that $u = 4$, $x = 2$, $z = 1$.

When $y = 3$ or 4, there are no solutions.

Therefore the solutions are: $(1, 1, 2)$ and $(2, 2, 1)$.

Problem 19. Solution: $(0, 1)$, $(1, 0)$, $(1, 2)$, $(2, 1)$, $(2, 2)$, $(0,0)$.

Note that all pairs of the form $(k, -k)$ are solutions, with integer k.

If $x + y = 0$, the equation becomes

$x^2 - xy + y^2 = x + y,$

which is equivalent to $(x - y)^2 + (x - 1)^2 + (y - 1)^2 = 2$. It follows that $(x - 1)^2 \le 1$ and $(y - 1)^2 \le 1$, restricting the interval in which the variables x, y lie to $[0, 2]$. We obtain the solutions $(0, 1)$, $(1, 0)$, $(1, 2)$, $(2, 1)$, $(2, 2)$.

It follows that $(x - 1)2 \le 1$ and $(y - 1)2 \le 1$, restricting the interval in which the variables x, y lie to $[0, 2]$. From here, we see that the following are solutions: $(0, 1)$, $(1, 0)$, $(1, 2)$, $(2, 1)$, $(2, 2)$. Note that $(0, 0)$ is also a solution.

Problem 20. Solution: $(1, 4, 12)$, $(1, 6, 6)$, $(2, 2, 3)$ and all their permutations.

The equation is equivalent to $1/x + 1/y + 1/z = 4/3$. Considering

$x \le y \le z$, it follows that $3 /x \ge 4/3$, i.e., $x \le 9/4$. Therefore $x \in \{1, 2\}$.

Analyzing the two cases, we obtain the solutions $(1, 4, 12)$, $(1, 6, 6)$, $(2, 2, 3)$ and all their permutations.

Problem 21. Solution: (A).

Method 1 (official solution):

The left member of the given equation can be factored into $m(m + 1)(m + 5)$ and rewritten in the form $m(m + 1)(m + 2 + 3) = m(m + 1)(m + 2) + 3m(m + 1)$.

For all integers m the first term is the product of three consecutive integers, hence divisible by 3, and the second term is obviously divisible by 3. So for all integers m, the left side is divisible by 3.

The right side, $3[9n^3 + 3n^2 + 3n] + 1$ has remainder 1 when divided by 3.
Therefore there are no integer solutions of the given equation.

Method 2 (our solution):
We consider the equation modulo 3:

$m^3 + 6m^2 + 5m = 27n^3 + 9n^2 + 9n + 1 \qquad \Rightarrow \qquad m^3 + 2m \equiv 1 \quad \text{mod } 3$

$\Rightarrow \qquad m^3 - m \equiv 1 \quad \text{mod } 3 \qquad \Rightarrow \qquad m(m^2 - 1) \equiv 1 \ \text{mod } 3$

$\Rightarrow \qquad m(m - 1)(m + 1) \equiv 1 \quad \text{mod } 3 \Rightarrow \qquad 0 \equiv 1 \quad \text{mod } 3$

Therefore there are no integer solutions of the given equation.

Problem 22. Solution: 495.

Method 1 (official solution):
The sum of nine consecutive integers is 9 times the fifth number, the sum of ten consecutive integers is 5 times the sum of the fifth and sixth numbers, and the sum of eleven consecutive integers is 11 times the sixth number. Thus any positive integer that can be written as a sum of nine, ten, and eleven consecutive positive integers must be a multiple of 9, 5, and 11. The smallest such number is 495. It is readily verified that

$$495 = 51 + 52 + \cdots + 59$$
$$= 45 + 46 + \cdots + 54$$
$$= 40 + 41 + \cdots + 50.$$

Method 2:
Let a be the number that can be expressed as the sum of 9, 10, and 11 consecutive integers.

$a = l + (l+1) + \cdots + (l+8) = 9l + 36,$

$a = m + (m+1) + \cdots + (m+9) = 10m + 45,$

$a = n + (n+1) + \cdots + (n+10) = 11n + 55,$

$l, m, n \in N$

Then $\begin{cases} 9l + 36 = 11n + 55, \\ 10m + 45 = 11n + 55. \end{cases}$

So $9l = 11n + 19$, $10m = 11n + 10$.

$$\begin{cases} l = n + 2 + \dfrac{2n+1}{9}, \\ m = n + 1 + \dfrac{n}{10}. \end{cases}$$

Thus $\begin{cases} 2n + 1 \equiv 0 \pmod{9}, \\ n \equiv 0 \pmod{10}. \end{cases}$

The smallest value for n is 40.

The smallest value of a is $40 + 41 + \cdots + 50 = 495$.

Note that AIME provided one solution to this 1993 problem and here we show you the second one.

Problem 23. Solution: 12.

$$kx = 72 + 3k \quad \Rightarrow \quad x = \frac{72}{k} + 3.$$

x is an integer only if k is a factor of 72. $72 = 2^3 \times 3^2$. The number of factors of 72 is $(2 + 1)(3 + 1) = 12$, so there are 12 values for k.

Problem 24. Solution: $x = 50$, $y = 7$.
The given equation can be written as
$$x^2 = 51y^2 + 1 = 49y^2 + 14y + 1 + 2y^2 - 14y = (7y + 1)^2 + 2y(y - 7).$$
When $y - 7 = 0$ or $y = 7$, the right hand side of the equation is a square number. Therefore the solutions are $x = 50$, $y = 7$.

Problem 25. Solution: $(0, 0)$, $(1, 0)$, $(0, 1)$, $(2, 1)$, $(1, 2)$, $(2, 2)$.
The given equation can be written as $x^2 - (y + 1)x + y^2 - y = 0$.
Since x is integer, we have
$$\Delta = (y + 1)^2 - 4(y^2 - y) \geq 0$$
Or $3y^2 - 6y - 1 \leq 0$
Or $\dfrac{6 - 4\sqrt{3}}{6} \leq y \leq \dfrac{6 + 4\sqrt{3}}{6}$ or

$$1 - \frac{2}{3}\sqrt{3} \leq y \leq 1 + \frac{2}{3}\sqrt{3}$$

Since y is integer, $y = 0, 1, 2$.

When $y = 0$, $x = x^2$ $\Rightarrow x = 0$ or $x = 1$.
When $y = 1$, $x^2 - 2x = 0 \Rightarrow x = 0$ or $x = 2$..
When $y = 2$, $x^2 - 3x + 2 = 0$ $\Rightarrow x = 1$ or $x = 2$.
The solutions are: $(x, y) = (0, 0), (1, 0), (0, 1), (2, 1), (1, 2), (2, 2)$.

Method 2:
The given equation can be written as
$$(x - 1)^2 + (y - 1)^2 + (x - y)^2 = 2$$
We have:

$$\begin{cases} (x-1)^2 = 1, \\ (y-1)^2 = 1, \\ (x-y)^2 = 0, \end{cases} \quad \begin{cases} (x-1)^2 = 1, \\ (y-1)^2 = 0, \\ (x-y)^2 = 1, \end{cases} \quad \begin{cases} (x-1)^2 = 0, \\ (y-1)^2 = 1, \\ (x-y)^2 = 1. \end{cases}$$

The solutions are:
$(x, y) = (0, 0), (1, 0), (0, 1), (2, 1), (1, 2), (2, 2)$.

Problem 26. Solution: $y = 5$ and $x = 6$.
Method 1:
Since we are finding positive integer solutions, $x > y$. Let $x - y = d$, so $x = y + d$.
The equation is equivalent to $3y^2 d + 3yd^2 + d^3 = y^2 + dy + 61$. We get
$(3d - 1)y^2 + (3d^2 - 1)y + d^3 = 61$. The last relation implies $d^3 < 61$; hence $d = 1, 2, 3$.
If $d = 1$, then $2y^2 + 2y + 1 = 6$, yielding $y = 5$ and $x = 6$.
If $d = 2$ or $d = 3$, the equation in y has no integral solutions.

Method 2:
Multiplying the equation by 27 and subtracting 1 from both sides, we obtain
$$(3x)^3 + (-3y)^3 + (-1)^3 - 3(3x)(-3y)(-1) = 1642.$$

The left-hand side is of the form $a^3 + b^3 + c^3 - 3abc$, and it factors as $(3x - 3y - 1)(9x^2 + 9y^2 + 1 + 9xy + 3x - 3y) = 2 \cdot 823$.

Since the second factor in the left-hand side is larger than the first, taking into account that 823 is a prime and that $3x - 3y - 1 \equiv 2 \pmod 3$, it follows that $3x - 3y - 1 = 2$ and that $9x^2 + 9y^2 + 1 + 9xy + 3x - 3y = 823$.
The solution is (6, 5).

Made in the USA
Lexington, KY
14 February 2017